P9-DFN-208

Assessing Preschool Literacy Development

Informal and Formal Measures to Guide Instruction

BILLIE J. ENZ
LESLEY MANDEL MORROW

Part of the Preschool Literacy Collection edited by
Lesley Mandel Morrow

INTERNATIONAL
Reading Association
800 Barksdale Road, PO Box 8139
Newark, DE 19714-8139, USA
www.reading.org

IRA BOARD OF DIRECTORS

The International Reading Association attempts, through its publications, to provide a forum for a wide spectrum of opinions on reading. This policy permits divergent viewpoints without implying the endorsement of the Association.

Executive Editor, Books   Corinne M. Mooney
Developmental Editor   Charlene M. Nichols
Developmental Editor   Tori Mello Bachman
Developmental Editor   Stacey L. Reid
Editorial Production Manager   Shannon T. Fortner
Design and Composition Manager   Anette Schuetz
Project Editor   Stacey L. Reid

Cover   Design, Monotype; Photograph, ©Masterfile

The publisher would appreciate notification where errors occur so that they may be corrected in subsequent printings and/or editions.

Library of Congress Cataloging-in-Publication Data
Enz, Billie.
   Assessing preschool literacy development : informal and formal measures to guide instruction / Billie J. Enz, Lesley Mandel Morrow.
      p. cm. — (Preschool literacy collection)
   Includes bibliographical references and index.
   ISBN 978-0-87207-690-7
   1. Language arts (Preschool)—Evaluation.   2. Educational tests and measurements.   I. Morrow, Lesley Mandel.   II. Title.
   LB1140.5.L3E69 2009
   372.6076--dc22   2008055379

With appreciation to all preschool teachers who know how to observe and assess their children, which guides their instruction.

CONTENTS

Billie Enz, PhD, is a Professor of Early Childhood Education in the College of Teacher Education and Leadership at Arizona State University in Mesa, Arizona, USA. She is a recognized expert in the area of new teacher development and mentor training, and has written several books about this topic, including *Trade Secrets for Primary and Elementary Teachers*; *Trade Secrets for Middle and Secondary Teachers*; *Ready, Set, Teach: A Blueprint for a Successful First Year*; and *Life Cycle of the Career Teacher*.

Currently Enz's major research focus is emergent literacy. She has coauthored two textbooks in this area: *Teaching Language and Literacy: From Preschool to the Elementary Grades* and *Helping Young Children Learn Language and Literacy: From Birth Through Preschool*. As a senior member of the Early Childhood faculty she teaches language and literacy courses and has recently codesigned an online master's program in early childhood education.

Enz is the past president of the Family Literacy and the Literacy Development in Young Children special interest group for the International Reading Association (IRA). She is also a member of IRA's Early Literacy Commission.

 Lesley Mandel Morrow is a Professor of Literacy at Rutgers University's Graduate School of Education in New Brunswick, New Jersey, USA, where she is chair of the Department of Learning and Teaching. She began her career as a classroom teacher, then became a reading specialist, and later received her PhD from Fordham University in New York City. Her area of research focuses on strategies for enhancing early literacy development and the organization and management of language arts programs. Her research is conducted with children and families from diverse backgrounds.

Morrow has more than 300 publications that include journal articles, book chapters, monographs, and books. She received Excellence in Research, Teaching, and Service awards from Rutgers University. She was the recipient of IRA's Outstanding Teacher Educator of Reading Award and Fordham University's Alumni Award for Outstanding Achievement. In addition, Morrow has received numerous grants for research from the U.S. federal government and has served as a principal research investigator for the Center of English Language Arts, National Reading Research Center, and the Center for Early Reading Achievement.

Presently, Morrow is a principal investigator for the Mid-Atlantic Regional Lab, funded by the U.S. Department of Education and New York University Medical School's BELLE Project: The Preparation of Disadvantaged Preschoolers for Language and Literacy Success during Pediatric Primary Care, funded by the National Institute for Child Health and Human Development. She was an elected member of the IRA Board of Directors and served as president of the organization in 2003–2004. She was elected into the Reading Hall of Fame in 2006.

GLOSSARY

This glossary provides definitions for many of the specialized literacy terms in this book. These terms are highlighted in boldface type on first occurrence.

alphabetic principle: The understanding that printed language consists of sentences, words, and letters, and that the letters consistently match to the sounds of spoken language.

anecdotal observation notes: The teacher records student interactions with peers, print, literature, writing process, in-class discussion, and center activities.

authentic assessment: Assessment based on activities that represent and reflect the actual learning and instruction in the classroom.

behaviorist model: A learning theory in which adults provide a model and children learn through imitation encouraged by positive reinforcement.

benchmarks/standards/milestones: Terms that refer to the content that preschool children are expected to be able to learn in preschool.

checklists: The teacher uses predetermined observation guides to document children's development on specific aspects of language or literacy behavior.

comprehension: An active process whereby a reader interprets and constructs meaning about the text based on prior knowledge and experience.

conferences: Discussions held with parents, children, or parents and children together in which the teacher discusses what the child has learned, what the child does well, and where the child needs improvement. Conferences should include suggestions for helping at home. Time needs to be left in the conference for parents to ask questions.

constructivism: A theory that views learning as an active process by which children construct knowledge to learn by problem solving, guessing, and approximating.

conventions of print: Understanding that writing is organized in a particular way (e.g., lists start at the top of the page and proceed downward; books are predictable and organized, with a cover, title, and author). Sometimes called *concepts about print* or *concepts about books*.

cultural diversity: Reference to the wide variety of backgrounds, languages, customs, and environments represented within the larger society or a given classroom.

daily performance work samples: Teacher collects student-created products to document each child's literacy development. All samples must have the child's name and date and a brief statement as to the objective of the lesson or a description as to why this piece was collected. Large products may be photographed. Articles that the children want to keep may be copied.

Directed Listening–Thinking Activity (DLTA)/Directed Reading–Thinking Activity (DRTA): Frameworks that offer directions and strategies for organizing and retrieving information from a text that is read by or to a child. The steps in DLTA or DRTA include preparation for listening or reading with prequestions and discussion, setting a purpose for reading, reading the story, and a follow-up postreading discussion based on the purpose set prior to reading.

emergent literacy: Term coined by Marie Clay that refers to a child's early unconventional attempts at reading, writing, and listening.

English-language learners (ELLs): Children whose first language is not English. These children can have varying levels of English ability, from no English to some.

environmental print (EP): Print that children see in the real-world environment, such as when they drive in the car or bus, as they shop with their parents in the store, or when they watch television. EP relies on stylized logos (colors, fonts, and format) for commercial toys or food products.

explicit instruction: A teacher-directed strategy with emphasis on teaching a task and the specific steps needed to master it. Also referred to as *direct instruction.*

expressive language: Putting words together to form thoughts or express oneself.

fluency: The ability to read with ease and rapidity or word recognition and articulation.

functional print: Print that is used to accomplish tasks or regulate behavior, such as stop signs or exit signs, or grocery lists or to-do lists.

graphic awareness: The awareness that print carries a message. When children "write" lists and letters or "play read" text using pictures and memory, they demonstrate an understanding of this concept.

high-stakes testing: Standardized measures or any one measure that makes major decisions about children's promotion or retention without using other information about the child.

learning centers: Spaces in the classroom filled with materials for independent student activity focusing on current topics of study within content areas and including literacy materials as well.

literacy center: A classroom area composed of a library corner and writing area.

onsets: The beginning parts of words, typically a consonant or consonant blend. For example, in the word *cat*, C is the onset.

parent-involvement programs: Programs designed to involve and inform parents about activities that will promote their children's literacy development in school.

phonemes: The individual sounds that make up spoken words.

phonemic awareness: The awareness that spoken words are composed of individual sounds, or phonemes.

phonics: The relationship between sounds and letters in written language.

portfolio assessment: A strategy for measuring student progress by collecting samples of student work that are placed into a folder called a portfolio. Materials include samples of student's written work or drawings, anecdotal records, audiotapes, videotapes, checklists, and teacher-made and standardized test results, among others.

print awareness: The ability to recognize print and the knowledge of concepts of print.

print- or literacy-rich environments: Environments rich with materials that encourage reading and writing and support instruction.

receptive language: The ability to process, comprehend, or integrate spoken language; being able to understand what someone says to you.

repeated reading: Reading the same book or story over and over until it is repeated or known. This familiarity offers the opportunity for fluent reading.

rimes: The ending parts of words, such as -*at* or -*an*. Also called *word families*.

rubrics: Scoring guides that define the level of performance that is expected. Rubrics serve as useful tools for students and teachers to get a sense of what they should strive for. They are often used in writing, reading fluency, and projects. An excellent sample is shown, as well as a good sample, and a poor sample. Then characteristics are stated for these samples. The same could be done for fluent reading, word recognition, color identification, and so on.

scaffolding: A strategy in which teachers provide children with modeling and support to help them acquire a skill.

self-assessment: Short questionnaires for students to discuss and talk about how they think they are progressing in a particular literacy area. For example, How do you think you are doing with writing your name? Where do you need some help?

shared book experiences: Whole- or small-group reading instruction through literature selections, in which Big Books are often used so that children can see the print and pictures. Big Books enable children to listen and participate in actual book readings.

small-group instruction: Close interaction occurs between teacher and child for explicit instruction, based on needs and interests and for assessment.

standardized tests: An assessment measure, commercially prepared and norm-referenced, that reports results in terms of grade-level scores and percentile ranks.

story retell: The recital of familiar stories, in children's own words, in written or oral form to develop and assess comprehension of story.

surveys and interviews: Students should be actively involved in assessing their own work, reflecting upon their progress, and establishing new learning goals. Likewise, parents can be involved in sharing information about student growth. To do this type of data collection, the teacher usually constructs a simple questionnaire. The form can be used to guide a conversation-style interview with either child or parent.

teacher observations: The basis for most student assessment. In all cases, the teacher labels, dates, and organizes observation records to document development over time.

t-unit: An independent clause with all its dependent clauses attached that is helpful in measuring a child's language complexity.

Very Own Words: Favorite words generated by children, written on index cards, and kept in a container for them to read and write.

word wall: A type of bulletin board or classroom display that features challenging and/or high-frequency words organized alphabetically.

CHAPTER 1

Multiple Assessments for Preschoolers

• • • • • • • • • • • • • •

Ms. Fine administers a standardized test to Darren. One of the activities is to circle the picture that shows a horse. The choices of pictures are a horse, a zebra, and a donkey. Darren has never seen a real horse; he has only seen them in pictures. Therefore, all three of these pictures look like horses to him. Darren circles all three pictures.

When the teacher works with Rosa on the same test, the child is confused. She has limited English skills and has been in her preschool class of 4-year-olds for only a few months. When the teacher asks the question, Rosa does not understand it, nor does she understand the directions about how to answer it. Rosa feels as though she has to do something, so she colors the three pictures.

• • • • • • • • • • • • • •

The preceding vignette demonstrates just two types of the problems that might be encountered when we formally test young children. While both children answered the questions incorrectly, each did so for a very different reason. Darren didn't have the experiential background to deal with the question in the way it was presented, and although Rosa's Spanish-language development was good, she did not understand the test since it was in English. What this information demonstrates is that teachers must view the incorrect answer as a starting point to gain insight into the child's instructional needs.

> Teachers must view the incorrect answer as a starting point to gain insight into the child's instructional needs.

In the past decade, there has been an emphasis on literacy instruction for preschool children that is intentional and systematic. This is especially true of children who attend Head Start and schools that qualify for Early Reading First Programs (Vukelich, Christie, & Enz, 2007). This new direction has been greatly influenced by research indicating how important quality preschool with an emphasis on language and literacy is for school achievement.

With the No Child Left Behind Act of 2001 and Early Reading First grants focusing on preschool literacy programs, there is a much greater emphasis on accountability than ever before. Therefore, this chapter deals with issues encountered by preschool teachers who face an increasing responsibility to account for children's achievement in literacy development. We introduce the topic of **authentic assessment** through **daily performance work samples** and **teacher observations**. In addition we discuss the appropriate uses of formal **high-stakes testing**. The practical applications for using both assessment and testing are discussed in the chapters that follow, which focus on the assessment of various specific language and literacy skills.

Assessing Early Literacy Development

> Assessment of children's growth and development is an essential component of all high-quality preschool programs.

Assessment of children's growth and development is an essential component of all high-quality preschool programs. Assessment allows teachers and parents to see how a child is progressing and helps teachers to prepare instruction appropriate for their students' ever-changing language development and literacy needs. Testing, on the other hand, enables teachers and program directors to evaluate how effective curriculum materials are for their children. Effective preschool teachers use both assessment and testing to inform their practice and provide specific information about student progress (Airasian, 2002).

Assessment and Testing Measures

So what are assessment measures and what are testing measures—and how are they different? *Assessment* includes systematic observations of student actions and the collection of student work. These informal observations, **anecdotal observation notes**, and artifacts are then synthesized, analyzed, and interpreted to help teachers make informed instructional decisions. On the other hand, *testing* involves formal, systematic, and standardized procedures for gathering samples of students' behavior. Children's progress is often compared with predetermined performance **standards** to ascertain a child's progress toward developmental **benchmarks** or **milestones**. Testing typically refers to a summative (final) evaluation that produces a numeric score or grade that summarizes a child's work for a semester or year. Assessment is information that is gathered on a daily or weekly basis that guides the teacher's understanding of how children are performing on a day to day basis. This information helps teachers to focus and adjust their instruction.

We begin here to simply introduce and describe multiple types of assessments and testing instruments. Later, in chapters that discuss tests and assessments for the major skill area—such as language development, concepts about and **conventions of print**, phonological awareness, **phonics**, **comprehension**, **fluency**, and writing—we provide actual samples of assessments and tests with vignettes describing how they are used in the classroom.

Frequently Used Types of Assessment

On-Demand Tests. On-demand tests occur during special time set aside for testing. In most cases, teaching and learning come to a complete stop while the teacher conducts the assessment.

Ongoing Assessment. Ongoing assessment, also called authentic assessment, relies on the regular collection of children's work to illustrate children's knowledge and learning. The children's products are created as they engage in daily classroom activities. Thus, children are learning while they are being assessed.

Authentic or ongoing assessment is a strategy that relies on the teacher's ability to systematically observe student actions and organize a collection of student work. These observations and artifacts are then synthesized and interpreted to help teachers make informed instructional decisions and to document student growth over time. *Authentic* refers to the way the data are collected—while the children are completing a real task during class activities. In other words, ongoing assessment "is the process of gathering information in the context of everyday classroom activities to obtain a representative picture of children's abilities and progress" (Dodge, Heroman, Charles, & Maiorca, 2004, p. 21). The artifacts (the children's work) are produced by the children while they engage in their daily classroom activities. The outcomes of these activities, then, serve the dual purposes of instruction and assessment. Because the children's artifacts are stored in portfolios, ongoing assessment is often called **portfolio assessment**. Because teachers are gathering samples of children's work to illustrate what the children know and can do, ongoing assessment sometimes is called work sampling.

Working Portfolios. A working portfolio is a folder in which both the student and teacher place work that is reflective of the student's achievement on a daily basis over time.

Showcase Portfolios. A showcase portfolio is a few carefully selected samples of student work that illustrate the student's efforts, progress, and achievements. The work represents all areas of literacy for which there are standards and objectives. This portfolio is shared with the child's parents and his or her teacher for next year (Gunning, 2003).

Frequently Used Types of Testing

Criterion-Referenced Tests. A criterion-referenced test is used to compare a student's progress toward mastery of specified content, typically content the student had been taught. The performance criterion is referenced to some criterion, such as a cut-off score of 60 required for mastery.

Norm-Referenced Tests. A norm-referenced test is designed to compare one group of students with another group.

Standardized Tests. A standardized test is one in which the teacher reads a verbatim script of procedures to the students. The conditions and directions are the same whenever the test is administered. Standardized tests are one form of on-demand testing.

Standardized tests are prepared by publishers and are norm-referenced. In other words, they are administered to large numbers of students to help establish norms. Norms are the average performance of students who are tested at a particular grade and age level. When selecting a standardized test, it is important to check for test validity; that is the determination that the test evaluates what it says it evaluates and matches the goals you have for your students. Test reliability is important as well; that is the determination that scores are accurate and dependable.

Other features of standardized tests are grade-equivalent scores, which are raw scores converted into grade-level scores. For example, if a child in preschool received a score equivalent to a kindergartner, his performance would be considered above grade level. Another feature is percentile ranks, which are raw scores converted into a percentile rank. They tell where the child ranked when compared with all children who took the test at his or her grade and age level. Therefore, if a child received a percentile rank of 80, it would mean that he or she scored better than or equal to 80% of all students taking the test at his or her grade and age level, and that 20% of the children taking the test scored better.

Although many criticisms are associated with standardized measures, they do present another source of information about a child's performance. Parents like receiving the information from the test because it is a concrete explanation of their child's ranking among others in the same grade. Realize, though, that standardized test results are just one type of information about a child that is no more important than all of the other measures discussed earlier. There are many questions about whether standardized tests should be used with very young children.

Concerns Associated With Standardized Testing

There are a number of problems associated with standardized tests, especially for preschool children. Again, we stress that standardized tests represent only one form of testing, and their use must be discussed in coordination with other assessment measures. Many feel that this type of test is inappropriate for preschool children, but the fact is that they are being used.

One of the most high-profile uses of standardized tests with preschoolers is the Head Start National Reporting System (NRS). The NRS assessments are standardized and measure a set of skills that include expressive and receptive English vocabulary, uppercase letter naming, and early math skills of size, shape discrimination, number identity and correspondence, and simple addition and subtraction. Teachers administer the NRS at the beginning and the end of each school year, and they are scored by an external organization that sends reports of overall program outcomes to Head Start and local administrations. The primary focus of the NRS is the overall progress that groups of children make in each Head Start program. The NRS is not designed to assess the school readiness of individual children (see www.govtrack.us/congress/bill.xpd?bill=h110-1429).

Some standardized tests for preschoolers evaluate children on skills such as auditory memory, rhyme, visual matching, and listening. By contrast, practices that nurture **emergent literacy** that may not be included in the test emphasize children's language development, prior knowledge, **graphic awareness**, letter recognition, association of meaning with print, and characteristics of printed materials. One child might pass all portions of a standardized test yet not be able to begin to read, whereas another child might not pass any portion of the test but is already reading. If teachers do not prepare children for the test they may not score well.

Aside from the content of the test, knowledge of how to take the test is crucial for success. Standardized tests are less reliable with younger children than with older children since these youngsters often don't understand the reason for the test, the test directions, and have trouble concentrating because of their short attention spans. Some standardized tests are still biased in favor of white, middle class children, as the language of the test reflects middle class vocabulary, despite genuine attempts to alleviate the problem. Their use can place rural, non-white, and bilingual youngsters at a disadvantage since they may not have the prior knowledge and experiences needed for successful achievement on the tests. In addition, following test directions such as "Put your finger on the star" or "Circle the goat that is behind the tree" is often a problem for the young child. Children who have never seen a goat may not circle anything because the animal on the page might look like a dog to them.

An Overview of Assessment Strategies

Assessment must be frequent and include many different types of data—including data from formal tests as well as informal assessments about children's progress on a daily basis. The main goal is to observe and record actual behavior that provides the broadest possible picture of a particular child. Preschool teachers who use a wide variety of assessments to collect information about children's literacy development provide the clearest picture of a child's knowledge. The following overview provides a glimpse of several data collection techniques. Subsequent chapters provide samples of each technique with suggestions about how teachers can use the data collection tools in their classrooms.

> Preschool teachers who use a wide variety of assessments to collect information about children's literacy development provide the clearest picture of a child's knowledge.

- *Teacher observations*: At the base of most student assessment is teacher observation. In all cases, the teacher labels, dates, and organizes observation records to document development over time.

- **Checklists**: The teacher uses predetermined observation guides to document children's development on specific aspects of language or literacy behavior.

- *Anecdotal observations*: The teacher records student interactions with peers, print, literature, writing process, in-class discussion, center activities, etc.

- *Daily performance work samples*: The teacher collects student-created products to document each child's literacy development. All samples must have the child's name and date and a brief statement as to the objective of the lesson or a description as to why this piece was collected. Large products may be photographed. Articles that the children want to keep may be copied.

- *Video/audio recordings*: The teacher documents students' ability to interact with peers, teachers, and parents; handle personal needs; mediate problems; and express their views. Language development, writing, knowledge about print, and comprehension can also be evaluated with video and audio recordings.

- **Surveys and interviews**: Students should be actively involved in assessing their own work, reflecting upon their progress, and establishing new learning goals. Likewise, parents can be involved in sharing information about students' growth. To do this type of data collection, the teacher usually constructs a simple questionnaire. The form can be used to guide a conversation-style interview with either child or parent.

- **Rubrics**: Rubrics are scoring guides and are useful tools for students and teachers to get a sense of what they should strive for. They are often used in writing. An excellent sample is shown, as well as a good and a poor example. Then characteristics are stated for these samples. The same could be done for fluent reading, word recognition, color identification, and so on.

- **Conferences**: Conferences are held with parents, children, and parents and children together. The teacher discusses what the child has learned, what they do well, and where they need improvement. Conferences should include suggestions for helping at home. Time needs to be left in the conference for parents to ask questions.

- **Self-assessments**: Self-assessments are usually short questionnaires for students to discuss and talk about how they think they are progressing in a particular literacy area; for example, "How do you think you are doing with writing your name? Where do you need some help?"

The International Reading Association (IRA) and National Association for the Education of Young Children (NAEYC) position statement *Learning to Read and Write: Developmentally Appropriate Practices for Young Children* (1998) suggests that when we evaluate young children's literacy development, procedures should be developmentally and culturally appropriate and based on the objectives for instruction. Evaluation should consider each child's total development and its effect on literacy performance. To remedy the abuse of standardized testing for example, don't make major educational decisions about a child based on this test score alone or any one measure. If this is done, it is referred to as high-stakes testing (IRA, 1999). The use of multiple assessment tools such as interviews, anecdotal records, and daily performance samples done frequently along with the **standardized tests** will present a total picture of a child's progress.

Therefore, we must remind teachers, parents, and administrators to understand that one measure—whether it be assessment or testing—cannot be the sole source for evaluating a child's progress. We will use these principles to guide our discussion throughout this book:

- The younger the child, the more difficult it is to obtain valid test results. Early development is rapid, episodic, and highly influenced by experience.
- Performance on a test may be affected by a child's physical condition, emotional state, and the conditions of the assessment or test on the day the test is administered.
- Assessment can be culturally sensitive and pose an alternative to testing but requires a lot of time in establishing criteria for judging development and evaluator training.
- Assessment is an ongoing process that includes collecting, synthesizing, and interpreting information about children, the classroom, and their instruction.
- Testing is one form of assessment that when appropriately applied can systematically measure literacy skills and instruction.
- While testing does not provide a complete picture, it is an important tool, for both its efficiency and ability to measure prescribed bodies of knowledge (Ruddell & Ruddell, 1995).

The following chapters offer preschool teachers and administrators explicit guidance in creating and using ongoing assessments tools to document student performance. Further, we will discuss how teachers can easily use this information to shape and refine future instruction. At the end of each chapter, we have included a feature called Professional Development, which provides options for teachers to consider as they continue to build their knowledge and skills. All teacher and student names used in this book are pseudonyms. Descriptions of students and teachers are composite sketches that represent real classroom situations that we have encountered in our studies.

PROFESSIONAL DEVELOPMENT

Discussing with other preschool teachers their evaluation system is a useful activity. At a study group session bring and share different materials and methods you use. Discuss what you like and don't like about each type of tool you use.

Review many other tests of various types that you can acquire to see what is available to evaluate preschool children's literacy development.

Discuss the pros and cons of daily performance samples, informal measures such as observations, and standardized tests.

Think about beginning a portfolio for a few of your students to have the opportunity to try out measures and evaluate what you like and don't like.

CHAPTER 2

Assessment-Guided Instruction

. . . .

Mrs. Ganesh is observing 4-year-olds Jade and Joy play together in the Alpha Land Center. The children are playing with coupons—Jade is sorting coupons and organizing them into categories. She says to Joy, "Look, I have six free Cokes."

Joy smiles and points to each coupon as she replies, "Well, really you have four Diet Cokes, a Pepsi—see the *P*? And a Mountain Dew—see the *M*?"

Mrs. Ganesh makes a brief anecdotal note describing what Joy and Jade know and can do. This information will also help her to adjust instruction to better meet both children's growing literacy knowledge. Actually, this scene inspires her to increase her use of the I Can Read bulletin board, for which the children bring in **environmental print (EP)** that they recognize. She realizes that the children are beginning to reinforce their knowledge of letters with the EP materials.

. . . .

As the preceding vignette illustrates, instruction and assessment are intertwined in excellent literacy instruction. The primary purpose of early childhood assessment, then, is to improve instruction. Figure 1 demonstrates the interaction between these essential aspects of teaching—instruction leads assessment and, in turn, assessment guides instruction. As Shepard, Kagan, and Wurtz (1998) note,

> When children are assessed as part of the teaching–learning process, then assessment information tells caregivers and teachers what each child can do and what he or she is ready to learn next. Finding out, on an ongoing basis, what a child knows and can do helps parents and teachers decide how to pose new challenges and provide help with what the child has not yet mastered. This type of assessment guides teachers' instruction. Teachers also use their assessment of children's learning to reflect on their own teaching practices so that they can adjust and modify curricula, instructional activities, and classroom routines that are ineffective. (p. 52)

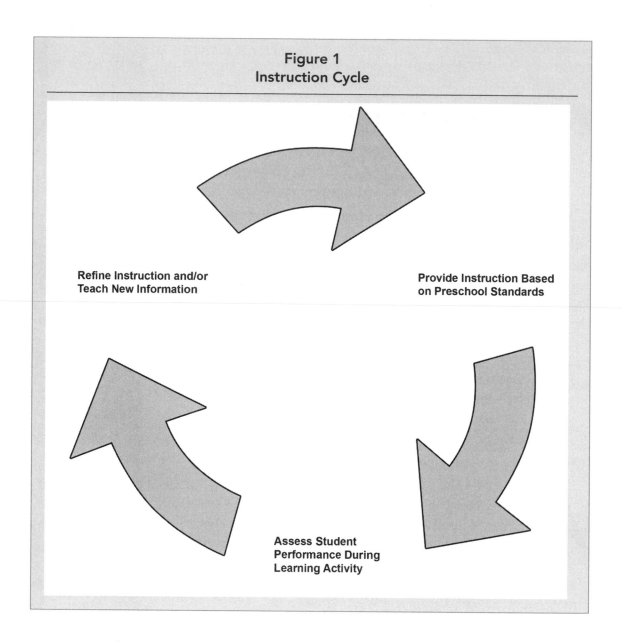

Figure 1
Instruction Cycle

Refine Instruction and/or
Teach New Information

Provide Instruction Based
on Preschool Standards

Assess Student
Performance During
Learning Activity

Research Support
for Assessment-Guided Instruction

In recent years, major studies (Committee on Education and the Workforce, 1999; Snow, Burns, & Griffin, 1998) have found that while the seeds of literacy are planted before children enter school, important literacy skills like knowledge about letters and sounds, print and pictures, words, and sentences are prerequisites for learning to read and write. Further, these studies indicate that these skills do not develop spontaneously: Instruction shapes them. Preschool teachers and day care providers, along with parents, must intentionally provide appropriate experiences and instruction to build this basic knowledge (Vukelich et al., 2007). These experiences include the following:

- Positive, nurturing relationships with adults who engage in responsive conversations with children, model reading and writing behavior, and foster children's interest in and enjoyment of reading and writing
- **Print-rich environments**, sometimes called literacy-rich environments, that provide opportunities and tools for children to see and use written language for a variety of purposes, with teachers drawing children's attention to specific letters and words
- Adults' daily reading of high-quality books to individual children or small groups, including books that positively reflect children's identity, home language, and culture
- Opportunities for children to talk about what is read and to focus on the sounds and parts of language as well as the meaning
- Teaching strategies and experiences that develop phonemic awareness, such as songs, finger-plays, games, poems, and stories in which phonemic patterns such as rhyme and alliteration are featured
- Opportunities to engage in play that incorporates literacy tools, such as writing grocery lists that are created in the dramatic play center or making signs in the block building center
- Firsthand experiences that expand children's vocabulary, such as trips in the community and exposure to various tools, objects, and materials

Preschool Language and Literacy Standards

Clearly, preschool children are capable of learning many literacy skills, and they relish learning to read and write when they are engaged in suitable and enjoyable activities (Gump, 1989). Teachers must begin the assessment process by determining what is appropriate for children to learn. Teachers must answer the following questions:

- What is important for us to know about our children's development as readers, writers, speakers, and listeners?
- What do these young learners need to know and be able to do when they exit the preschool years?

Today early childhood educators have a new resource to help them answer these questions. In nearly every state in the United States, teachers, educators, and parents have worked together to create language and early literacy (and mathematics, social and emotional development, science, social studies) standards that describe what language and literacy skills children should be able to learn. To support early literacy, the federal government, state agencies, and national organizations such as IRA and NAEYC (1998) have determined early language and literacy standards. These standards, sometimes called milestones or benchmarks, identify what children should know and be able to do after they receive appropriate literacy instruction. Figure 2 lists typical language and literacy standards for preschool classrooms.

Determining language and literacy standards is the first step; next these milestones must also be translated into everyday practice that easily and accurately allows teachers to observe and evaluate student performance and set teaching priorities.

Figure 2
Checklist of Language and Literacy Goals for Preschool Children

Listening Comprehension
__ Listens with increased attention
__ Understands simple oral directions
__ Listens to and engages in conversation

Speech Production and Discrimination
__ Identifies differences between similar sounding words (e.g., *tree* and *three*)
__ Produces speech sounds with increased ease and accuracy
__ Experiments with language

Vocabulary
__ Shows an increase in listening and speaking vocabulary
__ Uses new vocabulary in daily communication
__ Refines understanding of words
__ Increases listening vocabulary

(continued)

Figure 2 *(continued)*

Verbal Expression
__ Uses language for a variety of purposes
__ Uses sentences of increasing length and grammatical complexity
__ Uses language to express routines
__ Tells a simple personal narrative
__ Asks questions
__ Begins to retell stories in sequence

Phonological Awareness
__ Begins to identify rhymes
__ Begins to attend to beginning sounds
__ Begins to break words into syllables or claps along with each syllable
__ Begins to create words by substituting one sound for another

Print and Book Awareness
__ Understands that reading and writing are ways to obtain information and knowledge
__ Understands that reading and writing communicate thoughts and ideas
__ Understands that illustrations carry meaning but cannot be read
__ Understands that letters are different from numbers
__ Understands that a book has a title and an author
__ Understands that print runs from left to right and top to bottom
__ Begins to understand basic print conventions (e.g., letters are grouped to form words, words are separated by spaces)

Letter Knowledge and Early Word Recognition
__ Begins to associate letter names with their shapes
__ Identifies 10 or more printed letters
__ Begins to notice beginning letters in familiar words
__ Begins to make some letter sound matches
__ Begins to identify some high-frequency words

Motivation to Read
__ Demonstrates an interest in books and reading
__ Enjoys listening to and discussing books
__ Requests being read to and re-reading the same story
__ Attempts to read and write

Knowledge of Literary Forms
__ Predicts what will happen next in a story
__ Imitates special language in a book
__ Asks questions about the information or events in a book
__ Connects information and events in books to real life

Written Expression
__ Attempts to write messages
__ Uses letters to represent written language
__ Attempts to connect the sounds in a words with its letter forms
__ Begins to dictate words and phrases to an adult who records it on paper

Teacher Observations and Checklists That Guide Instruction

The following example follows one preschool teacher, Mrs. Gleason, as she does the following:

- Determines instructional activities (based on the Arizona preschool literacy standards)
- Designs an authentic assessment as part of the instructional activity
- Uses this information in a classroom performance matrix to determine further instruction
- Collects student artifacts to document individual student growth

· · · · · · · · · · · · · · · ·

As Mrs. Gleason plans her lessons she also considers how her 18 young prekindergarten students will be able to demonstrate their new knowledge. For the past month she has introduced six alphabet letters and sounds using many exciting activities to help the children become alphabet detectives and sound sleuths. During this week she has organized a letter center activity that not only reinforces these new skills but also serves as an authentic assessment of the children's knowledge.

To accomplish this goal, she plans to have the children do a letter hunt using environmental print coupons and labels the children (and their parents) have collected. She has created a worksheet to help document the children's efforts (see the completed Alphabet Activity Assessment in Figure 3). The children are to sort through the pile of coupons until they find the target letters, and then they will glue them in the appropriate row. Mrs. Gleason and her aide are a part of this center and make notes on the children's actions as they complete this assignment. The notes are collected over the course of the week as the children rotate through the centers during class (see the Alphabet Matrix in Figure 4). The information from the matrix allows Mrs. Gleason to see at a glance which child knows what letters and then determine who needs further instruction.

· · · · · · · · · · · · · · · ·

Figure 3
Alphabet Activity Assessment

Name **A n n i e** Date _____

Please write the letter in the box. Find pictures and words from your coupons that start with this letter. Glue the pictures and words in the row.

B		
B	**Barbie**®	
F	FR☺☺T L☺☺PS	
P	⊙ PEPSI	

Figure 4
Alphabet Matrix

Key for each row.
1. Student wrote the letter correctly
2. Student recognizes letter immediately
3. Student knows the letter sound

Student	B	F	P	T	M	R	Comments
Annie	+	+	+	+	+	+	• Great improvement printing letters
	+	+	+	+	+	+	• Recognizes letters in words—even some lowercase
	+	+	+		+	+	• Knows most of the letter sounds
							• Followed directions well
							• Shared materials easily with peers
Briar	+	+	+	+	+	+	• Prints letters extremely well, rapidly
	+	+	+	+	+	+	• Recognizes all letters
	+	+	+			+	• Letter sounds are improving
							• Followed directions
							• Shared materials
Callie	+	+	+	+	+	+	• Enjoys printing letters; form is improving
							• Knows most of the letter names
							• Still needs additional work time with letter sounds
							• Had difficulty following directions
							• Shared materials

Notice that Mrs. Gleason is accomplishing several standards, including the following:

Listening comprehension
- Listens with increased attention
- Understands simple oral directions

Letter knowledge and early word recognition
- Begins to associate letter names with their shapes
- Identifies 10 or more printed letters
- Begins to notice beginning letters in familiar words
- Begins to make some letter-sound matches

Written expression

- Attempts to connect the sounds in words with their letter forms

To begin planning her lesson, Mrs. Gleason uses her school district's curriculum goals. During the first semester of prekindergarten, the curricular emphasis is on learning letters and letter sounds. To teach these concepts, Mrs. Gleason designs instructional activities that double as student assessments. To teach the alphabet, Mrs. Gleason uses environmental print logos. The children's instant recognition of the logos allows her to focus their attention on the initial letters and the sounds they make.

The children have created environmental print alpha charts and sort the logos by initial alphabet letter. The children have brought logos in since the first week of school and are now able to recognize several letters. To verify their skill, Mrs. Gleason designs a worksheet (artifact) that requires children to recognize their letter, print the letter, and glue a logo that represents that letter on their paper. She will be able to collect information about the children's progress as she observes them completing the activity using the checklist she has developed. Likewise, since this is a social activity, Mrs. Gleason will be able to relay how well each child is working with peers.

Since the children's activity worksheet displays their work, their work can then be placed in their progress portfolio to document their progress over time. For example, Annie's work shown in Figure 3 demonstrates an earlier version of this assessment only had three letters, but the next version of this assessment will have 9, then 12. Mrs. Gleason selects the letters to be included on the assessment based on new letters she has presented and specific target letters that provided a challenge for the students initially. Her assessment of the children provides immediate feedback about the effectiveness of past lessons and helps her to design new lessons for tomorrow. The comments are written at the table as the children play the game.

Currently Mrs. Gleason uses a simple worksheet to compile this information, but she is learning how to collect this same information on her laptop, using a spreadsheet. This new approach will allow her to manipulate the data easily and produce immediate class and individual progress reports.

This simple assessment and learning activity demonstrated to Mrs. Gleason that though most of her students knew the letters and their names, they were still learning the letter sounds and needed more instruction in forming the letters. This caused her to add an additional letter-sound game to her lesson plans and to ask her aide to work more closely at the writing center to demonstrate and reinforce letter writing. Likewise, during shared writing time she decided to take a few moments to highlight the features of target letters.

Clearly, authentic assessment of young children is the best indication of what they actually know and are able to do, but again it is important for the teacher to be able to document this information to share with directors, colleagues, and parents.

As this chapter reveals, planning instruction and assessment simultaneously requires the teacher to be aware of the state standards for preschool children. This knowledge helps teachers to target the appropriate curricula and design interactive instruction. Likewise, teachers are able to see if their instruction is effective in helping children learn these expected skills. In the following chapter we discuss how teachers can organize their learning environment using learning centers that help the children learn and practice new knowledge and skills.

In subsequent chapters we will review methods for teaching and assessing the following:

- Language development
- Phonological awareness and early phonics
- Concepts about print and writing
- Assessing comprehension and concepts about books

> Authentic assessment of young children is the best indication of what they actually know and are able to do, but again it is important for the teacher to be able to document this information to share with directors, colleagues, and parents.

PROFESSIONAL DEVELOPMENT

One way teachers determine what they want and need to know about children's literacy development is by reviewing national, state, and local standards. Search the state's website or contact the state or a school district to obtain a copy of the state or local standards of language arts.

Design a lesson plan and highlight the standards you will be teaching and assessing. Create an assessment checklist or design a learning activity that also serves as an assessment artifact.

CHAPTER 3

Assessing the Preschool Literacy Environment

The physical environment of a classroom, including the arrangement of space, choice of materials, and the aesthetic quality created, are essential ingredients for successful learning in preschool. The literacy-rich classroom is filled with meaningful language experiences and materials that encourage exploration (Morrow, 2005). However, preparing a classroom's physical environment is often overlooked. Frequently, we concentrate on lesson planning and forget to give equal consideration to spatial arrangements in which teaching and learning occur. Yet it is crucial that the curriculum and environment are coordinated to create the most effective literacy instruction.

In this chapter, we describe what an exemplary literacy-rich preschool environment looks like and then provide evaluation tools to determine if your own environment includes important elements that support your literacy instruction. The description is a composite of preschool classrooms that were observed over a long period of time. As we speak of the teachers, keep in mind that the discussion is based on a collective profile of several who were identified as exemplary. This synthesis of findings from expert teachers enables us to present a description of an exemplary literacy-rich preschool classroom environment (Pressley, Rankin, & Yokoi, 1996).

Research Support for Carefully Designed Environments

Historically, theorists and philosophers emphasized the importance of the physical environment in early learning and literacy development. Pestalozzi (cited in Rusk & Scotland, 1979) and Froebel (1974) described the preparation of manipulative materials that would foster literacy development in real-life environments. Montessori (1965) advocated a carefully prepared classroom environment to promote independent learning and recommended that each kind of material in the environment have a specific learning objective. She prepared her classroom with materials that were accessible to children.

Research has shown ways in which the physical design of the classroom affects the children's behavior (Loughlin & Martin, 1987; Morrow, 1990; Rivlin & Weinstein, 1984). Rooms partitioned into smaller spaces, such as centers, have facilitated verbal interaction among peers and have enhanced cooperative and associative learning. When rooms are carefully designed for specific types of instruction, such as a table for meeting with a small group of children, there is more productivity and greater use of language than in rooms where no attention is given to setting (Moore, 1986).

Literacy-rich environments stimulate activities that enhance literacy skill development (Morrow, 2005; Neuman & Roskos, 1992). Story props, such as puppets or a felt board with story characters, improve story production and comprehension, including recall of details and the ability to interpret text (Morrow, 2002). Researchers have found that children like cozy corners with pillows and rugs to retreat to when things get hectic, and opportunities for privacy are important for children who are distractible and for those who have difficulty relating to peers (Weinstein, 1981; Weinstein & Mignano, 1996). Young children work best in rooms with variation; that is, they have warm and cool colors, some open areas and cozy spots, as well as hard and soft surfaces (Olds, 1987).

The nature and quality of the literacy environment plays a central role in literacy learning and the acquisition of literacy behaviors and attitudes. Chall, Jacobs, and Baldwin (1990) observe, "No one will debate the idea that a rich literacy environment is helpful for achievement in literacy" (p. 162).

Research over the last two decades has provided plentiful and pertinent information about the design and implementation of print-rich classroom environments (Holmes & Cunningham, 1995; Neuman & Roskos, 1997, 2002; Taylor, Blum, & Logsdon, 1986). Despite the widespread acceptance and awareness among teachers and children and the abundance of research information available, the findings of current research indicate that implementation of "print-rich classroom environments" is lagging well behind what is known and available (Neuman & Roskos, 1997). Teacher educators, teachers, and school administrators need to understand at a deeper intellectual level how to assess the design of classroom literacy environments if they are to enlarge their understanding of what a print-rich classroom environment includes.

With the support of appropriate materials and a well-designed class-room environment, instruction will flourish in preschool classrooms. Evaluate and assess the richness of your literacy environment and make it as important as the literacy curriculum. If this is done they will support each other during instruction.

The Physical Environment in Exemplary Preschool Classrooms

Exemplary preschool classrooms are arranged so that they are "student friendly" (Vukelich & Christie, 2009). Materials are stored for easy access both visually and physically. The teachers use a variety of materials that enable them to accommodate and address the different abilities and inter-ests of their children. For example, one of the classrooms we visited was in the basement of an old inner city school and was by no means picturesque; however, the ingenuity of the teacher made the environment quaint, warm, and inviting. It had adequate space for 18 children, good lighting, and it was kept clean. In this classroom and in many of the classrooms studied, the children's tables are arranged close together so that 4 or 5 youngsters sit together, which encourages social interaction. The rooms have provisions for whole-group instruction with students sitting at their tables or on a rug in the literacy center. In the area for whole-group meetings, there is a chalk-board and/or white board, a pocket chart, and an easel with experience chart paper. Teachers have rocking chairs they use when doing whole-class minilessons or reading stories to the children.

Exemplary classrooms all have morning meeting areas that include **functional print** such as a calendar, weather chart, helper chart, and rules for the classroom. Signs communicate information, such as "Quiet Please" and "Please Put Materials Away After Using Them." Environmental print with logos from the real world—such as traffic signs and familiar clothing and food chains—are important to display as well. All print should have some type of picture or logo to help children understand what is written. The rooms have notice boards used to talk with the children through writ-ing. In addition, there are **word walls**. The children's names are the most prominent words on the word walls as well as words dealing with current themes being discussed (e.g., animals in the forest or plants). There are other materials in the room representing the units being studied, such as children's literature, books made by the class, and artwork. An alphabet chart is on the wall, but at eye level for children to see.

The teachers we observed all have arranged their rooms for small-group and one-on-one teaching (see Figure 5). There is a table situated in one side of the room. At this table, the teacher meets with small groups and individual children, based on need, for **explicit instruction** in literacy. The teacher has all the materials needed for skill instruction available in this

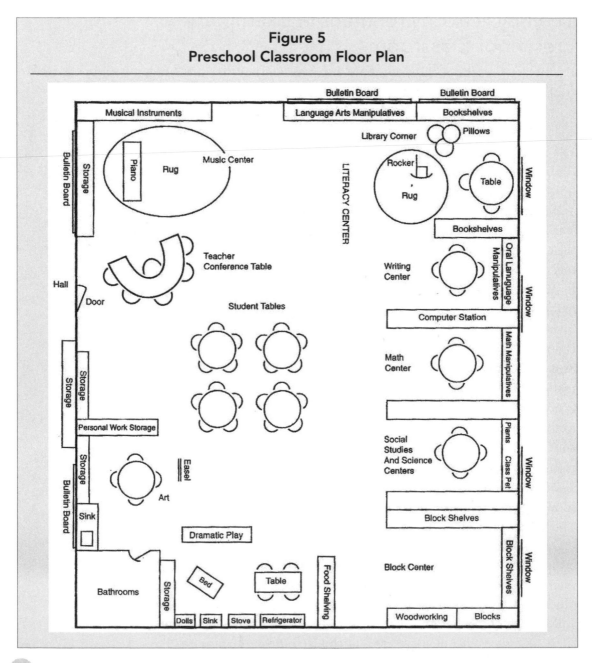

Figure 5
Preschool Classroom Floor Plan

area. These include a pocket chart, an experience chart, individual writing slates, and magnetic boards with magnetic letters for dealing with knowledge about print and writing. In addition, there are theme-related books, and folders to assess and record student accomplishments and needs. There are corrugated cardboard bins, labeled with children's names, where children store individual work. These materials are packaged in zip lock baggies. (See Morrow, Freitag, & Gambrell, 2009, and Vukelich & Christie, 2009, for further guidance on effective floor plans and classroom setup.)

Learning Centers

To accommodate small-group, independent work, there are **learning centers**—each labeled according to content areas (see Figure 5). The centers integrate literacy learning into content areas by featuring reading and writing activities. Therefore, it is common to find paper and pencils in the block and dramatic play area, and books in the art and music centers. They use themes such as the family, the community, or seasons for developing new vocabulary, new ideas, and purposes for reading and writing. Each of the centers has general materials that are typical of the content they represent, but also special materials added that are linked to the current thematic topics of study and literacy materials as well. Some examples of centers found in exemplary teachers' classrooms are outlined here.

The Dramatic Play Center

This center includes dolls, dress-up clothing, a play telephone, stuffed animals, a mirror, food cartons, plates, silverware, newspapers, magazines, books, a telephone book, cookbooks, notepads, and a kitchen setting with a table and chair. The area will have a broom, dustpan, refrigerator, storage shelves, and a theme that changes with the theme studied. For example, we often found restaurants from different multicultural backgrounds in the dramatic play area such as one month a Chinese restaurant with a menu, recipes, a cash register, play money, and checks. This changed to an Italian restaurant after a while with a new appropriate menu.

• • • • • • • • • • • • • •

Darlene and Jamal are pretending to be a Mom and Dad going to the supermarket. "Now let's make a list for the supermarket. I have the pencil and paper. What do we need?" asks Darlene. "We need more Sugar Pops cereal; we are all out of it."

Jamal says, "That's not so good for your teeth and we will get fat from all of that sugar. We have to find another cereal. Just write down cereal. Here it says it on this box. You can copy it."

"I know," says Darlene. "We can get some cereal bars. They taste good and my mommy said they are good for you. They have protein and other good stuff."

The children were studying good nutrition, and what they were learning was being assimilated into their play. The materials in the environment and some modeling and **scaffolding** by teachers encouraged this productive activity.

• • • • • • • • • • • • • • •

The Music Center

This area includes a piano, guitar, or other real instruments (see Figure 5). There are also rhythm instruments such as bells, triangles, rhythm sticks, cymbals, and instruments from different countries, such as maracas from Mexico and a Caribbean steel drum. There are CD and tape players with music that links to themes, such as songs about the different seasons. In one classroom, for example, the teacher selected "Rain Rain Go Away" and "If All of the Raindrops Were Lemon Drops and Gumdrops" when studying spring. This was the rainy season in the area where these children lived. The children learned new vocabulary in these songs and selected some for their word wall; they drew rain pictures and had the teacher label them as they wished, or they wrote their own labels. The rain pictures became a class book.

The Art Center

This center includes easels and multiple types of paper in different sizes. There are colored pencils, markers, watercolors, and collage materials (such as pipe cleaners, foil paper, wool, and string fabrics) in order to account for all types of creative artwork. Depending on the theme, different materials will be added. For example, in one classroom play dough was added when studying zoo animals, and children chose an animal they wished to create. There are books with illustrations of animals for children to look at to help with their designs. There are labels so the children can give their animals names and write the types of animals they made.

The Social Studies Center

This center is particularly important for themes such as the study of different cultures or family, friends, and the community. These themes focus on getting along with others, recognizing and appreciating differences and likenesses in friends and family, developing respect for self and others, and developing a community of learners. Appropriate books accompany these ideas. In addition, some general social studies materials include maps, a globe, flags from various countries, community figures, traffic signs, current events, and artifacts from other countries.

The Science Center

This center is always popular; it should include interesting objects to explore and experiment with, such as magnets, simple machines, and plants. Other equipment includes an aquarium, terrarium, thermometer, compass, prism, shells, rock collections, stethoscope, kaleidoscope, and microscope. In all of the rooms we observed, a theme was studied and materials that represented that theme were present. The following is an anecdote from Ms. Casey's preschool classroom, where they designed a veterinarian's office as part of a science theme on pets. When observing this classroom we saw children using oral language they had not used before; they pretended to read and write materials and words they had never heard before.

· · · · · · · · · · · · · ·

The dramatic play area is designed as a waiting room with chairs; a table filled with magazines, books, and pamphlets about pet care; posters about pets; office hour notices; a no-smoking sign; and a sign advising visitors to "Check in with the nurse when arriving." A nurse's desk holds patient forms on clipboards, a telephone, an address and telephone book appointment cards, a calendar, and a computer for recording appointments and patient records. Offices contain patient folders, prescription pads, white coats, masks, gloves, cotton swabs, a toy doctor's kit, and stuffed animals to serve as patients.

Ms. Casey guides students in the use of the various materials in the veterinarian's office, for example, by reminding the children to read to pets in waiting areas, fill out forms with prescriptions or appointment times, or fill out forms with information about an animal's condition. In addition to giving directions, Ms. Casey also models behaviors by participating in play with the children when the materials are first introduced. She observes the children at play to record their behavior to see that they are engaged in productive literacy play.

• • • • • • • • • • • • • • •

The Math Center

Children will find an abacus, varied types of currency, scales, rulers, measuring cups, clocks with movable parts, a stopwatch, calendar, cash register, calculator, a number line, height chart, hourglass, different types of manipulative numbers (felt, wood, magnetic), fraction puzzles, and geometric shapes in their math center. The units that will be studied in this preschool program will include activities emphasizing measuring in "Growing Like Me," and recording numbers of members in "My Family and My Community."

Block Area

In the block center we find many different sizes, shapes, and textures of blocks, figures of people, animals, toy cars and trucks, and items related to themes being studied, such as tractors for a unit on building. Books about the themes are useful for constructing theme-related structures, and paper and pencils are needed to make signs to label constructions created by the children.

The Literacy Center

The **literacy center** should be one of the focal points in a preschool classroom. It should give the message that literacy is so important that a special spot is made to provide space for writing, reading, oral language, listening, comprehension, and word-study materials, as well as time to use this space.

In this area, there is a rocking chair and rug because many of the activities in this center take place on the floor, and it is where the teacher has group meetings, lessons, and story time. There are pillows and stuffed animals to add an element of comfort.

Books are stored in open-faced shelving for displaying titles about themes being studied. These books are changed with the themes and for featuring special selections. Books are also stored in plastic baskets that are labeled by genre, such as books about animals, seasons, poetry, families, and so on. Pictures accompany the labels.

Well-stocked preschool classroom libraries have 5 to 8 book selections per child at about 3 or 4 different levels of difficulty. The books included in the center are picture storybooks, poetry, informational books, magazines, biographies, cookbooks, joke books, folk tales, and fairy tales. Children enjoy books with real information as well as narrative stories. Therefore, you should have an equal number of both fiction and nonfiction books on hand. Books can be acquired over time, by purchasing them at flea markets, through points gained from book club sales, through donations from parents, and by using allotted classroom budgets. The teachers rotate their books regularly to maintain children's interest in them and children can check books out of the classroom to read at home. Literacy manipulatives such as puppets, taped stories with headsets, and felt boards with story characters, and electronic stories, are included in the literacy center to engage children through different modalities dealing with books. The story manipulatives help children learn to retell stories, and are an excellent comprehension strategy and assessment tool. The literacy center also has a shelf of manipulative materials that offer practice in concepts about print. These materials, which include matching games, rhyming games, magnetic, wood, and felt letters, help children learn the alphabet, phonemic awareness, and some sound–symbol relationships.

A portion of the literacy center called the Author's Spot is set aside and includes a table, chairs, and writing materials such as colored markers, crayons, pencils, chalk, a stapler, a hole punch, a chalkboard, and a white board. There are various types and sizes of paper such as newsprint, mural paper, lined paper, and colored paper. Classrooms should have bookbinding machines for making class books. Children are provided with journals and their use is supervised to ensure appropriate use. There are index cards used for recording children's **"Very Own Words,"** which are stored in index boxes. Folders, one for each child, are used to collect writing samples. Classrooms have about two computers in each room that are in good working order with excellent software for writing and reading activities.

Teachers prepare blank books for children to write in that relate to themes being studied. For example, there are different animal-shaped books when studying animals, or books shaped like snowmen and flowers to represent different seasons for that topic of study. There is a place for children to display their written work, a mailbox, stationery, envelopes, and stamps for children to write to each other and to pen pals.

Assessing Your Classroom Environment

Observations of preschool children working in literacy centers help the teacher to evaluate if the setting is conducive to the type of activity planned for the students. Teachers can assess student engagement in literacy behavior. The following vignette provides that type of evaluative information.

• • • • • • • • • • • • • • • •

Isabela and Veronica are using the felt board and story characters for "The Three Bears," taking turns retelling the story while looking at the pages of the book and putting the figures up on the felt board at the appropriate times. When they come to repetitive phrases in the story such as "Who's been sitting in my chair?" they say them together.

Matthew and Gabriel are at the author's table looking at snake books and drawing pictures and copying words from the book while they discuss the characteristics of the snakes. "This one is green and has a pointing tongue," says Matthew. Gabriel responds, "This one has big sharp teeth."

Tashiba has multiple copies of a story the class heard read by the teacher several times. She hands out the copies to the other children and keeps one for herself. She makes a circle of chairs where the group then sits as she pretends to be the teacher. She pretend-reads to the others. She asks the children questions about the story when she is done reading.

• • • • • • • • • • • • • • • •

Isabela and Veronica comprehend the basic story and can tell it in a sequence. Matthew and Gabriel understand that a book creates meaning and contains pictures and print, while Tashiba understands that books are for reading and that when you read a story it is important to talk about it.

Everything in these rooms has a function, a purpose, and a place for it to be stored. Exemplary teachers model new materials, their objectives for using the material, how they are used, and where they belong. Early in the school year, there are only a few items in the centers so the children can learn to use them properly. The teacher adds to them slowly as different themes and skills are studied.

The classrooms observed used philosophies and practices regarding classroom materials, and the organization of space from current and historical perspectives about learning. In addition teachers established clear rules, routines, and expectations for behavior. The children and their teachers decide upon the rules, practice them early in the school year, and are consistent in adhering to them on a day-to-day basis (Weinstein & Mignano, 1996). The teacher communicates the rules and expectations in a supportive manner, showing respect for students at all times.

The plan for the physical environment described is used based on the assumption it supports and enhances instruction. Evaluate and assess the richness of your literacy environment using the checklist in Figure 6.

The Classroom Literacy Environmental Profile (CLEP)

Wolfersberger, Reutzel, Sudweeks, and Fawson (2004) developed the Classroom Literacy Environmental Profile (CLEP), a tool for examining the "literacy richness" of early childhood and elementary classrooms. These researchers identified, defined, and organized into categories through a literature reviews, classroom observations, and teacher focus groups the multiple characteristics of literacy-rich classroom environments.

CLEP is composed of 33 total items and 2 subscales. Subscale 1 focuses on the quantity and organization of print materials and literacy tools available in the classroom. Subscale 2 focuses on the organization and literacy interactions using print materials and literacy tools in the classroom. Each of the 33 items is rated on a 7 point Likert-type rating scale with descriptors under points 1, 3, 5, and 7. When using the CLEP instrument, subscale 1, to examine early childhood and elementary language arts classroom literacy environments, examiners rate the following:

> (1) the quantity, utility, appropriateness of literacy-related objects or tools; (2) the quantity of genres, levels, format, and content of text materials; (3) classroom organization print, (4) student literacy product displays, (5) reference materials available; (6) forms of written communication; (7) writing utensils, (8)writing surfaces, (9) publishing supplies, and (10) technology available. To examine the organization of "literacy rich" language arts classrooms using subscale 2, users of the CLEP instrument assess (1) storage, organization, classroom space allocations by size, location, boundaries, and types; (2) the presence of a classroom library; (3) grouping and accessibility of reading and writing tools; (4) invitations and encouragements to participate in literacy events; (5) authentic literacy events, settings; interactions with literacy tools; (6) variety of literacy products produced; and (7) sharing of literacy products.

Figure 6
Checklist for Evaluating and Improving the Literacy Environment

Literacy Center
__ Manipulatives (roll movie or puppets with related books)
__ Children participate in designing the center (develop rules, select a name for center, and develop materials)
__ Area placed in a quiet section of the room
__ Visually and physically accessible, yet partitioned from the rest of the room
__ Rug, throw pillows, rocking chair, bean bag chair, and stuffed animals
__ Private spot in the corner, such as a box to crawl into and read
__ The center uses 10% of the classroom space and fits 5 or 6 children

The Library Corner
__ Bookshelves for storing books with spines facing outward
__ Organizational system for shelving books
__ Open-faced bookshelves for featured books
__ 5-8 books per child
__ Books represent 3 to 4 grade levels of the following types:
    (a) picture books, (b) picture storybooks, (c) traditional literature,
    (d) poetry, (e) realistic literature, (f) informational books,
    (g) biographies, (h) chapter books, (i) easy to read books,
    (j) riddle/joke books, (k) participation books, (l) series books,
    (m) textless books, (n) television-related books, (o) brochures,
    (p) magazines, (q) newspapers
__ 20 new books circulated every 2 weeks
__ Check-out/check-in system for children to take out books daily
__ Headsets and taped stories
__ Felt board and story characters with the related books
__ Materials for constructing felt stories
__ Other story manipulatives
__ System for recording books read (e.g., cards hooked onto a bulletin board)

The Writing Center (The Author's Spot)
__ Tables and chairs
__ Writing posters and a bulletin board for children to display their writing by themselves
__ Writing utensils (pens, pencils, crayons, felt-tipped markers, colored pencils)
__ Writing materials (many varieties of paper in all sizes, booklets, and pads)
__ Typewriter or computer
__ Materials for writing stories and making them into books
__ A message board for children to post messages for the teacher and students
__ A place to store "Very Own Words"
__ Folders for children to place samples of their writing

Wolfersberger and colleagues (2004) assert that CLEP is a valid and reliable tool for evaluating the literacy–richness of early childhood classrooms to enrich, refine, and redesign classrooms to foster engaged literacy learning for all children. In addition, the authors of CLEP suggest that the instrument may also serve as a reliable guide for educators to apply a more calculated approach to the design of literacy enrichments.

Student Interviews

Another way to assess your classroom environment is simply to talk to your students. Results from such interviews found that physical environment has a substantial effect on children's learning and development. Holmes and Cunningham (1995) found that very young preschool children, ages 3–4, evidenced a keen awareness of their classroom environments. These researchers found that children could, by looking at classroom photographs, identify appropriate activities for spaces in the classroom, as well as draw their classrooms representing these activity spaces. In another study, Kershner and Pointon (2000) asked 70 5- and 6-year-old children questions using the Individualized Classroom Environmental Questionnaire, which allows children to express their views about their classroom environments as places for working and learning. The children expressed strong views about grouping schemes, seating arrangements, wall displays, general tidiness, noise levels, and choices to work alone or in collaboration with others, to name only a few.

PROFESSIONAL DEVELOPMENT

- In a study group, discuss special features in your classroom you believe enhance the literacy environment. You will be surprised what you learn from your peers. One teacher said she put a little lamp in the literacy center and it made it feel more like a room at home. Another said she included a plant, and still another said she put her gerbils there since her children read to them.
- Think about your entire room and make a floor plan of what you have now. Then figure how you might make it better to give you more space for literacy center activities.
- Check your room with the CLEP instrument to see where you excel and where you need improvement. Finally visit other preschool teachers' rooms to learn from them about ideas they have found useful for storage, **small-group instruction** space, and so on.

CHAPTER 4

Assessing and Enhancing Language Development

• • • • • • • • • • • • • •

Four-year-old James tells his preschool teacher that he and his grandma looked at the moon last night and his grandma said it was "full." James asks his teacher, "Why was the moon full, did he eat too much for dinner?" James has used his background knowledge related to the word *full* to help him understand what had been said. Until this time, the word *full* meant filled up with food. His teacher explains what was meant by a full moon and that the same words can have different meanings depending on the situation in which they are used.

Children learn language in an active manner by constructing it. In another preschool class, the discussion is about what the children want to be when they grow up. Michael says he wants to be a doctor like his dad, because he visited the operating room where his dad works and he liked the machines. He says, "When I grow up, I want to be an operator, just like my Daddy." Michael has reconfigured the word *operate* to make sense of the situation.

• • • • • • • • • • • • • •

Language acquisition is based somewhat on developmental maturity, but children play an active role by constructing language, as illustrated in the preceding vignette. They imitate adult language and create their own when they do not have the conventional words they need. When their attempts are positively reinforced, they are motivated to continue generating language. Children who are exposed to rich language and have the opportunity to use it with adults and children in a social context develop more facility with language than children who don't have the opportunity (Adams, Beeler, Foorman, & Lundberg, 1998; Cazden, 2005; Dickinson, McCabe, Anastaspoulos, Peisner-Feinberg, & Poe, 2003; Gaskins, 2003; Morrow, 2005; Morrow, Kuhn, & Schwanenflugel, 2006).

In this chapter, we discuss how language is acquired from birth through age 6, as well as strategies that teachers and parents can use to encourage development; however, the main purpose of the chapter is to demonstrate how to assess language development, in what settings, and what these assessments mean for instruction.

Knowing How Children Acquire Language Helps With Assessment

> To evaluate language, one must know how it is acquired and what is expected for development at different ages.

To evaluate language, one must know how it is acquired and what is expected for development at different ages. According to the **behaviorist model**, adults provide a language model and children learn through imitating that model. The child's language acquisition is encouraged by positive reinforcement (Cox, 2002; Hart & Risley, 1999). For example, when newborns coo, parents are delighted and respond with words of encouragement, so the infant responds to the positive reinforcement by repeating the cooing sounds. As babies put consonant and vowel sounds together such as *ba, ba, ba,* or *ma, ma, ma* at about 8 months of age, parents may perceive this as the child's first words. The adult encourages the baby and says, "Now say it again, *ma, ma, ma.*" Pleased by the warm response, the baby repeats the sounds.

Constructivism describes language as an active and social process in which children are the creators. As children construct language, they often make errors that help them learn how language works (Brown, Cazden, & Bellugi-Klima, 1968). For example, a 4-year-old described his new jacket as having "*French fries* hanging on the sleeves"; he was referring to the fringe.

According to Halliday (1975), children's initial language development is based on relevance and function. In other words, what can be said reflects what can be done. The following are the functions of language identified by Halliday (pp. 19–21):

- *Instrumental*: Children use language to satisfy a personal need and to get things done. (Example: "Cookie Mommy.")
- *Regulatory*: Children use language to control the behavior of others. (Example: "No sleep now.")
- *Interactional*: Children use language to get along with others. (Example: "You want to play?")

- *Personal*: Children use language to tell about themselves. (Example: "I'm running now.")
- *Heuristic*: Children use language to find out about things, to learn things. (Example: "What are cows for?")
- *Imaginative*: Children use language to pretend, to make believe. (Example: "Let's play space.")
- *Informative*: Children use language to communicate information of others. (Example: "I'll tell you how this game works.")

As children develop, they discover the rules that govern the structure of language—specifically, those of phonology (sounds in words), syntax (grammar), and the meaning of words, called semantics (Berk, 1997; Pflaum, 1986). There are stages of language development, but the pace of development differs from child to child. Knowing what to expect from a child in terms of language development can help us assess if the child's language is developing as it should.

Understanding Stages of Language Development for the Purpose of Assessment

From birth to 1 year, language acquisition begins. In infancy, oral language consists of a child experimenting or playing with sounds. Infants cry when they are uncomfortable and babble, gurgle, or coo when they are happy. Infants learn to communicate needs by producing different cries. Parents are usually able to distinguish cries; one cry is for hunger and another is for pain. When babies are about 8 months old, their babbling becomes more sophisticated. They are usually capable of combining a variety of consonant sounds with vowel sounds. They often repeat these combinations over and over. The repeated consonant and vowel sounds, such as *da, da, da*, sound like real words and parents will positively reinforce the child's behavior. Through repetition of specific sounds and continued reinforcement, the child begins to associate making a particular sound with the meaning of the word the sound represents.

From 12 to 18 months, a child's comprehension of language far exceeds that child's ability to produce it. Children do, however, start speaking their first words which are meaningful to them, such as *Mommy, Daddy, bye-bye, baby, cookie, milk, juice,* and *no*. As they become experienced with their first words, children use holophrases—one-word utterances that express an entire sentence (Hart & Risley, 1999). For example, a baby might say, "Cookie," but mean "I want a cookie," "My cookie is on the floor," or "I'm done with this cookie."

From 1 to 2 years of age, a child utters many sounds with adult intonation as if speaking in sentences. These utterances are not understandable. Children begin to use telegraphic speech at 12 months. Telegraphic speech uses content words, such as nouns and verbs, but omits function words, such as conjunctions and articles. However, the words are delivered in correct order, or syntax: "Daddy home" for "Daddy is coming home soon," or "Toy fall" for "My toy fell off the table." By 18 months, most can pronounce four-fifths of the English phonemes and use 20 to 50 words (Bloom, 1990).

From 2 to 3 years of age, the average child experiences dramatic language development. A child's oral vocabulary grows from 300 words to 1,000. The child can comprehend but cannot yet use 2,000 to 3,000 additional words. Telegraphic sentences of 2 or 3 words continue to be most frequent, but syntactic complexity continues to develop and the child occasionally uses functional words such as pronouns, conjunctions, prepositions, articles, and possessives. Children play with language by repeating new words and making up nonsense words. They enjoy rhyme and repetition (Bloom, 1990). Consider the following transcription of Tyler (2 years, 10 months) with his cat: "Nice kitties, my kitties, white kitties, furry kitties, good kitties, kiss kitties." Tyler's language is repetitive, playful, silly, and creative.

From 3 to 4 years of age, a child's vocabulary and knowledge of sentence structure continues to develop rapidly. Children add plurals, and regular verbs top their repertoire. Children of this age are prone to over-generalization in using these two structures, mainly because both plural formation and verb inflection are irregular in the English language (Jewell & Zintz, 1986). Four-year-old Keith illustrated both problems when he said, "I dropped a block on my foots and hurted myself." Keith knew how to form a plural by adding an *s* to *foot* and the past tense of a verb by adding *ed* to *hurt*, but he did not know about irregular plurals such as *feet* and irregular verbs such as *hurt*.

At age 4, children seem to have acquired all the elements of adult language. They generate language and apply rules that govern it; for example, while playing with play dough, Jonah said to himself, "I'm pounding the yellow play dough. I'm rolling it and cutting it. I'm making a birthday cake." Although Jonah sounds as if he is using adult speech, he has acquired only the basic foundations. Language continues to grow throughout our lives (Seefeldt & Barbour, 1986).

From 5 to 6 years of age, children sound even more like adults when speaking. They have vocabularies of approximately 2,500 words and are extremely articulate. Many, however, still have difficulty pronouncing some sounds (Newberger, 1997). The language of 5- and 6-year-olds is interesting, amusing, to the point, and delightful (Seefeldt & Barbour, 1986). They talk a lot and use language to control situations. Their language reflects their movement from a world of fantasy to a world of reality.

Assessment and objectives for language development are the same. We need to follow objectives for language instruction from birth to age 6 to teach, assess, and then teach more as a result of what we determine from the assessments. The two types of language we are concerned about are receptive and expressive language. **Receptive language** is language that is heard and hopefully understood. **Expressive language** is a child's oral language.

Objectives for receptive language development

- Provide children with a setting where they hear varied language.
- Provide children opportunities to associate language with pleasure and enjoyment.
- Expose children to a rich source of new vocabulary on a regular basis.
- Have children listen to others and demonstrate that they understand what is said.
- Provide children with opportunities to follow directions.
- Provide children with good models of English.
- Allow children to hear their home language in school.

Objectives for expressive language development

- Encourage children to pronounce words correctly.
- Help children increase their speaking vocabularies.
- Encourage children to speak in complete sentences.
- Provide children with the opportunity to expand on their syntactic structures, such as adjectives, adverbs, prepositional phrases, dependent clauses, plurals, past tense, and possessives.
- Encourage children to communicate so they can be understood.

- Give children the opportunity to use language to interpret feelings, points of view for solving problems, summarizing events, and predicting outcomes.

- Provide children with the opportunity to develop mathematical and logical relations, by using language that enables them to describe size and amount, compare, and define sets and reason.

- Provide children with the opportunity to talk in many different settings: in the whole group with the teacher leading the discussion; in teacher-led small groups; in child-directed groups for learning; or in conversation in social settings.

- Give opportunities for children to use their own language freely at any stage of development. This could be a different dialect or mixtures of English and Spanish.

- Encourage, accept, and respect children's communication.

- Ensure that language is integrated with other communication skills and embedded within topics or content areas that have meaning and function for children.

Assessment of Children's Language Development

When we assess children's language, we determine if it follows expected stages of development, how much a child has progressed, and what the instructional needs are. Assessment suggests several frequent measures by which to judge progress. Assessment should reflect language objectives and the use of skills in multiple contexts. One child may perform better in an interview than when trying to get a language sample with an audio recording. Many kinds of evaluation should be used because of performance differences and because the scope of almost any measure is not broad enough. Some concepts to use when assessing language are as follows:

- Select assessments that reflect your instruction.

- Incorporate student self-assessment with teachers, parents, and other students.

- Assess words students need to know.

> When we assess children's language we determine if it follows expected stages of development, how much a child has progressed, and what the instructional needs are.

- Assessment should be systematic, especially when it comes to vocabulary.
- Assess both receptive and expressive (oral) language.
- Use several measures and assess frequently.

Informal Assessment Measures

There are many ways to measure children's language development—we describe several of these informal measures here.

Checklists. Checklists are practical because they provide concise outlines for teachers. They are most effective if used 3 or 4 times during the school year. Program objectives offer criteria to include on checklists such as the one provided in Figure 7.

Anecdotal Observation Notes. Anecdotal observation notes provide a rich source of information about language development. Use a loose-leaf notebook or file for keeping anecdotal records. These records require no particular format. The teacher writes down incidents or episodes when they occur. Many samples of a child's language and situations in which they occur are recorded to determine growth over time (Au, 1998).

Audio and Video Recordings. Audio and video recordings can be done either in the form of an open interview or when children are unaware that their conversation is being recorded; when children are unaware of the recording, they are likely to be uninhibited, which may make the sample more authentic (Genishi & Dyson, 1984; McGee, 2007; Otto, 2006). It is helpful to make the recording device a familiar tool used in the classroom so it is not threatening when used for assessment.

To record samples of natural language, discuss the child's experiences. Ask about home, favorite games or toys, favorite TV programs, brothers and sisters, trips taken, or birthday parties. You should try to collect a corpus of spontaneous language that provides a typical sample of the child's ability. Audio and video recordings can be used to determine language development and comprehension of story through retellings. They can be used in discussions to help reveal how youngsters participate and the types of responses they offer. Video allows you to see a child in action. Labeled recordings are easily stored in a child's portfolio.

Figure 7
Checklist for Language Development Skills

Child's Name _____ Date _____

Expressive Vocabulary	Always	Sometimes	Never	Comments
Makes phoneme sounds				
Pronounces words correctly				
Can be understood by others				
Has appropriate vocabulary for maturity level, which increases daily				

Listening Vocabulary	Always	Sometimes	Never	Comments
Identifies familiar sounds				
Differentiates similar sounds				
Understands the language of others when spoken				
Understands stories read				
Follows verbal directions				
Listens to and engages in conversation				

Verbal Expression	Always	Sometimes	Never	Comments
Uses language for a variety of purposes				
Tells simple personal narrative				
Can retell stories heard				
Asks questions				
Speaks in one-word sentences				
Speaks in two-word sentences				
Speaks in complete sentences				
Uses sentences of increasing length				
Uses varied syntactic structures				

Record audio assessment samples a few times a year. Let children hear their recorded voices and enjoy the experience. Transcribe the recordings and analyze them for numbers of words uttered, numbers of different words, and words spoken in a single connected utterance (for example, "Tommy's cookie" or "Me want water"). Length of utterance is considered a measure of complexity, and the length of such utterances can be averaged to determine mean length. When children begin to speak in conventional sentences such as "That is my cookie," measure the length of the **t-units**. A t-unit is an independent clause with all its dependent clauses attached, assuming it has dependent clauses. It can be a simple or complex sentence. Compound sentences are made up of two t-units. Length of t-units, like length of utterances, is a measure of language complexity. It typically increases with age and usually the more words per unit, the more complex the unit (Hunt, 1970).

Further analysis of taped utterances and t-units can determine which elements of language a child uses: number of adjectives, adverbs, dependent clauses, negatives, possessives, passives, plurals, and so on. The more complex the syntactic elements, the more complex the language (Morrow, 1978). Figure 8 provides a corpus of language from a 5½-year-old preschooler at the end of the year, divided into t-units. She was asked to tell a story from the pictures in a book. There are 20 t-units in the sample in Figure 8 with a total of 130 words. The number of words per t-unit is 5.1. Earlier in the school year this same child had an average t-unit length of 4.2 in a similar language sample. The number of words per t-unit is a fairly reliable indicator of language complexity since there may be more adjectives or adverbs in the t-unit or dependent clauses making the sentence more syntactically complex.

Standardized Language Development Assessments

Thus far the assessments for language development described have been informal measures, but there are also many formal assessment measures in the form of standardized tests. The Boehm Test of Basic Concepts, Preschool (third edition) and The Peabody Picture Vocabulary Test: 2 Years to 18 Years are tests that determine children's vocabulary development and their use of complex sentence structure (McGee, 2007).

The standardized measures only allow for one test at the beginning of the year and one at the end. They have norms, reliability, and validity factors associated with them. It must be remembered that at the time it is given, a young child may not feel well, may not pay attention, might be tired, etc. One measure should never be used as the only assessment for major academic decisions, and both informal and formal assessments should be used simultaneously. Descriptions of well-known standardized tests for young children are provided here.

The Preschool Language Scale 4 (PLS–4). This formal assessment has an extended span of language skills and norms to capture a better picture of a child's language ability. Norms for this edition include a research base on a larger, more diverse sample of children, including those with disabilities, and more than one-third of this sample is of an ethnic minority. It has a Spanish edition with new norms. Furthermore, experts around the country have critiqued the PLS–4 to make sure the items are appropriate for children of different economic and cultural backgrounds. All language skills items have been well-researched and scrutinized. For children from birth to 2.11 there are more items targeting interaction, attention, and vocal/gestural behaviors. For 5- and 6-year-olds, there are more items targeting early literacy and phonological awareness, which is a good indication of school readiness. The PLS–4 also includes a Caregiver Questionnaire for parents/caregivers to share the child's communication in the home. The PLS–4 incorporates parents' information into the child's norm-referenced scores. You can find more information online at harcourtassessment.com/HAIWEB/Cultures/en-us/Productdetail.htm?Pid=015-8659-406&Mode=summary.

The Test of Language Development (TOLD). TOLD is an individually administered assessment that examines the language skills of children ages 4–12. This oral test is primarily used to reveal strengths and weaknesses of a child's language development, as well as to diagnose major language disorders, such as mental retardation, speech delays, and articulation problems. There are two levels of assessment depending on the children's ages: The Primary Version assesses children between 4–8.11 years. There are seven subtests in the following areas: Picture Vocabulary, Oral Vocabulary, Grammatic Understanding, Sentence Imitation, Grammatic Completion, Word Articulation, and Word Discrimination. The results are reported in terms of standard scores, percentile rankings, age equivalents, and a language quotient. In the more recent years, TOLD has been refined to incorporate a larger demographic of students, with separate studies for minority and disability groups. You can find more information online at ags.pearsonassessments.com/group.asp?nGroupInfoID=a19075 or at findarticles.com/p/articles/mi_g2602/is_0005/ai_2602000526.

Boehm–3 Preschool. This is an individually administered assessment for children ages 3.0 to 5.11 designed to evaluate young children's understanding of the basic concepts important for language and cognitive development and later success in school. The relational concepts as defined by Boehm–3 Preschool include size, direction, position in space, time, quantity, classification. There is also a Spanish edition. The test provides information to speech-language pathologists, preschool educators, school psychologists, and educational diagnosticians. The Boehm–3 Preschool has two levels: one assessment for children ages 3.0 to 3.11. On this test there are 52 items representing 26 concepts, most of which are tested twice. The second level is designed for children ages 4.0–5.11. This test also includes 52 items corresponding to 26 concepts. The Boehm is recognized for its reliable and accurate results since it has undergone stringent quality control measures in the standardization process including a determination that items are fair to all students—meaning that ethnic and gender bias has been addressed. You can find more information online at www.pearsonassess.com.

Fox in the Box. This assessment is useful in identifying primary students at risk and offers innovative tools for assessing K–12 literacy. It takes approximately two or three weeks to administer this test. About 30 minutes is spent on each child for one-on-one activities and there are small group activities that total about 80 minutes. The activities, which involve a friendly fox-puppet, help evaluate the children's literacy skills and help meet their individual needs. It is a fun, engaging way of having the children interact while doing these activities. The concepts measured in this test are phonemic awareness, phonics, reading and oral expression, and listening and writing. The Fox in the Box reduces performance anxiety for children with the help of the puppet; it includes a training video for easy administration, and has individual progress records and student folders, a Teachers Guide, and 12 books to help determine each child's level of reading achievement. Fox in the Box targets the literacy needs of children in the early stages of learning. You can find more information online at ags.pearsonassessments.com/group.asp?nGroupInfoID=a19075 or at canadiantestcenter.com/products/FoxInTheBox.asp.

The Woodcock Johnson Tests of Achievement (WJ III). This is designed to measure intellectual abilities and academic achievement. The test is for those from 2 to more than 90 years of age. This current edition of the test updates and expands the previous edition (WJ-R) by combining the intention to identify an individual's strengths and weakness with the intention to measure general and specific cognitive functions. Testing for these things together allows the tester to identify over- or underachievement and find patterns of inconsistency among individuals across different cognitive and achievement areas. Scores are reported while testing, and these raw scores are converted into age and grade equivalents, percentile ranks, and discrepancy scores using the Scoring Tables. The scores help determine an individual's ability to speak English in informal and academic settings. The results of reliability and validity are relatively high and consistent, which influence the decision-making of the test process. The norm samples taken consisted of preschool students, grade school students, college students, and adults. They were chosen on a variety of factors including location, race, SES, occupation, sex. More information can be found online at alpha .fdu.edu/psychology/woodcock_ach_descrip.htm or at www.riverpub .com/products/wjIIICognitive/pdf/asb-1.pdf.

Assessment of Literacy and Language (ALL). This instrument is used to detect early signs of language impairments that might later lead to difficulty reading. This assessment is administered to children in preschool, kindergarten, and first grade as individuals or in groups. It assesses both verbal and written language in specifically the following areas: listening comprehension, language comprehension, semantics, syntax, phonological awareness, alphabetic principles, and concepts about print. There are various other subtests that assess children's language skills. For instance, one subtest is Parallel Sentence Production, where the teacher describes a picture using certain grammar, and then the student describes a similar picture using the same grammatical structure the teacher did. This tests the student's syntax and morphemic knowledge. ALL is a useful tool for identifying language disorders, language development deficiencies, and weak language acquisition in the earlier years of a student's education process. More information can be found online at www.pearsonassess.com or at www.sedl.org/cgi-bin/mysql/rad.cgi?searchid=202.

Peabody Picture Vocabulary Test (PPVT–III) Expressive Vocabulary Test. The PPVT–III is an untimed, individually administered oral assessment that is used to measure an individual's sensory vocabulary for English. The PPVT–III can be used to identify non–English-speaking individuals' verbal ability. Thus, this test works for a range of language backgrounds. For the process of administering this test, the examiner provides a series of pictures for each individual. There are 4 pictures on a card and each picture is numbered. The examiner says a word that describes one of the pictures, and the individual is to point or say the number of the picture that is associated with the word. This test can be administered quickly (10–15 minutes); it has national norms, clear drawings, no reading or writing required for the examinee; items have been reviewed by a multicultural panel; and the scoring is objective and rapid. More information can be found online at ags.pearsonassessments.com/group.asp?nGroupInfoID=a12015.

Language Development Activities That Support Assessment From Birth to Age 2

When we assess language we need to know appropriate strategies to help develop a child's needs. We do this from specific research-based strategies that provide insight into what children learn and need to learn. Although this book is focused on preschool-age children, it is important to have an understanding about what happens, or should happen, developmentally with children before they become older and formally begin learning language and developing literacy.

Activities to Support Children's Oral Language Development From Birth to Age 2

Different parts of the brain are responsible for different kinds of development. The Wernicke's area is responsible for language understanding and the Broca's area for speech production. The first year of life is the most critical time for language to be learned. At birth, a child has neurons waiting to be connected for every language in the world. Neuron shearing occurs as early as 6 months of age when the baby can no longer recognize sounds of languages they have not heard (Kuhl, 1994). By 1 year old, a child is programmed to listen to and learn the language the child has heard, and is no longer programmed for those the child hasn't been exposed to; those neurons no longer remain. What does this mean for families and child care providers who are engaged with children from birth to age 3? From the time of birth through age 3, family members and child care providers need to do the following:

- Provide love, food, and clothing for babies.
- Talk to babies from the day they are born.
- Use sophisticated vocabulary with babies.
- Use complex sentences with babies.
- Respond to babies' cries, smiles, etc.
- Be playful with language, such as using rhymes.
- Play with babies.
- Read books to babies.
- Sing songs to babies.
- Play many different types of music for babies to hear.

At home or in day care, infants need to be surrounded with happy sounds and language experiences such as chanting nursery rhymes, finger plays, and songs. Adults can make up their own chants to make them meaningful for the children. In addition to conversation, infants should experience a variety of music types. Read to babies, since they need to hear the sounds of "book language," which is a source that can enhance language growth. Talk about sounds that provide practice in auditory discrimination, such as the doorbell ringing, the teapot hissing, the clock ticking, a dog barking, a bird singing, etc. Bring them to the baby's attention, give them names, and heighten the child's sensitivity to them (Lindfors, 1989).

Surround infants with sensory objects since they need to see, touch, smell, hear, and taste. Objects should be placed in the baby's crib or playpen. The objects will stimulate activity and curiosity. Some of the objects should make sounds or music when pushed or touched. They can have different textures and smells. They should be easy to grab, push, kick, or pull. They should be visible and within the child's reach. Suspend items overhead such as stuffed animals, rubber toys, and mobiles that hang from the ceiling and rotate by themselves. Books can be propped open against the side of the crib or playpen when the baby is lying on his or her back, or against the headboard when the baby is on his or her stomach. Allow the child to play independently with these objects; however, adults need to talk about them, name them, and join the child in playing.

From 6 to 12 months, the baby gurgles, coos, begins to laugh, and babbles. Adults or caregivers should recognize an infant's sounds as the beginning of language and positively reinforce the infant with responses aimed at encouraging the sounds. When the baby begins to put consonants and vowels together, again adults should reinforce the behavior, imitating what the baby has uttered and urging repetition. Soon the baby becomes aware of the ability to repeat sounds and control language output. Babies will also begin to understand adult language, so it is important to name objects, carry on conversations, and give the baby directions. At the end of its first year, assuming he or she has experienced appropriate sounds of language, encouragement, and pleasant interaction, the baby will be on the verge of extensive language growth during his or her second year.

One method for helping a child develop language is to model or scaffold (Applebee & Langer, 1983). In scaffolding, an adult provides a verbal response for a baby who is not capable of responding on his own. When the baby says "dolly," for instance, the adult responds, "Here is your pretty dolly." In addition to expanding on the child's language, the adult can extend it by asking the youngster to do something that demonstrates understanding and extends his or her thinking. For example, "Can you hug the dolly? Let me see you hug her." Assuming the child does hug the doll, he or she is demonstrating language comprehension. Adults can ask questions that require answers of more than one word, such as, "Tell me what your dolly is wearing." *How* and *why* questions encourage more than a yes or no answer, while *what*, *who*, and *when* questions elicit only one-word replies.

New experiences help develop language. For 1- to 2-year-olds, frequent outings, such as visits to the post office, supermarket, and park provide experiences to talk about and new concepts to explore. Involving them in household tasks enriches children's language. For example, an 18-month-old can put a piece of laundry into the washing machine or give one stir to the bowl of food being prepared. During these experiences, use language and identify new objects for the baby, and ask for responses related to each activity (Hart & Risley, 1999).

> New experiences help develop language.

Materials for language development should be varied. Toys in the home or day care center should include items of various textures, such as furry stuffed animals and rubber balls. Other toys should require simple eye–hand coordination. Three- to five-piece puzzles, trucks that can be pushed and pulled, dolls, a child-size set of table and chairs, crayons and large paper, and puppets are other examples. Toys should encourage exploration, use of the imagination, and the need to communicate. The number of books in a child's library should be increasing and accessible.

Activities to Support Children's Oral Language Development From Ages 3–5

For teachers to develop and assess language, children need opportunities to use materials that they can touch, smell, taste, feel, look at, and then talk about as they interact with other children and the teacher. Exploring and experimenting alone, with peers, and under the guidance of the teacher or parent are all situations that need to occur for language to flourish. Children need the opportunity to use language in preschool that involves creative expression, imagination, problem solving, and decision making. From ages 3 to 5 years, a great deal of language develops. Children need to hear good models, have opportunities to use language in social situations with adults and other children, and have their language production positively reinforced and assessed.

Activities can be repeated throughout the school year with new themes studied. Such adaptation and repetition make it possible to introduce children to hundreds of new vocabulary words, concepts, and ideas. For purposes of assessment, note the difficulty of the words children are asking for, not the words they use in their retellings and stories they create.

Different organizational structures in classrooms will provide different types of talk experiences. Teachers can provide directed question-and-answer discussions, small-group conversations to give and receive information, and spontaneous discussions that are led by the teacher or children. In structured discussions, teachers need to provide open-ended questions that will encourage talk, such as "What would happen if…? What would you do if…? Tell us why." Conversations occur best in small groups that include 3 to 6 children. Children need time to talk without leaders also. This type of conversation is likely to occur during free-play periods, center time, or during outdoor play. Although classrooms that encourage this type of talk can be noisy, it is important for children to use language in these social settings.

Whether the conversations are with or without the teacher, teacher talk needs to be kept to a minimum. The teacher should, however, redirect conversations if they stray from a designated purpose. Children need to learn the following guidelines about engaging in conversations:

- Listen to others.
- Take turns talking.
- Raise your hand if necessary to ensure everyone gets a turn.
- Listen; do not interrupt.
- Keep talk relevant to the topic of conversation.

Language should be purposefully integrated into active meaningful experiences with other content areas such as art, play, math, and social studies, rather than taught separately. To accomplish this, teachers must provide excellent strategies and exciting materials. They organize centers of learning, one for each content area. Teachers should keep records of discussions that take place in these centers. A checklist can be used for assessing language development in these settings; audio and video tapes should be made as well.

Dramatic play is a perfect venue for developing and assessing language. When designed to promote literacy learning, the dramatic play area can be coordinated with a social studies or science theme to bring meaning to the experience. Materials for reading and writing are provided to support the play theme, and, during play children read, write, speak, and listen to one another using literacy in functional ways. Although early childhood educators have realized the value of play for social, emotional, and physical development, in the past it has not been viewed as a place or time to develop and assess language and literacy. Children can be observed in this setting for their engagement in social collaborative meaningful language and literacy activities (Morrow, 1990; Neuman & Roskos, 1992).

To demonstrate the importance how much language will occur and be able to be recorded and observed, we will visit Ms. Hart's classroom of 4-year-olds.

· · · · · · · · · · · · · · ·

Ms. Hart designed a veterinarian's office with an animal theme. The dramatic play area includes a waiting room with magazines, books, and pamphlets about pet care, and posted office hours. A nurse's desk has patient forms on a clipboard, a telephone, an address and telephone book, appointment cards, a calendar, and a computer for recording appointments and patient records. Offices contain patient folders, prescription pads, white coats, masks, gloves, cotton swabs, a toy doctor's kit, and stuffed animals to serve as patients.

Ms. Hart models behaviors for students in the use of the materials in the veterinarian's office. She reminds them to read to pets in waiting areas, or fill out forms with information about an animal's condition.

During their play, Jessica tells her stuffed animal dog Sam not to worry, that the doctor won't hurt him. She asks Jenny, who was waiting with her stuffed animal cat Muffin, what the kitten's problem is. After talking a while, the girls pretend to read to their pets.

Preston, the veterinarian, examines Christopher's teddy bear and writes a report. He reads his scribble writing and says, "This teddy bear's blood pressure is 29 points. He should take 62 pills an hour until he is better, keep warm, and go to bed."

· · · · · · · · · · · · · · ·

As the teacher observes children in dramatic play settings, he or she can assess how they use language, how they listen and respond, and the vocabulary they select. The dramatic play area can be changed from a kitchen to a grocery store, a gas station, an airport, a post office, a business office, a restaurant, etc. Include reading, writing, and other appropriate materials related to the theme of the center (Morrow & Rand, 1991).

Sharing children's literature is another activity that helps develop and assess oral language development. Research studies have found that children who are read to frequently and who are included in discussions about the stories before and after reading develop sophisticated language structures and increased vocabulary (Beck & McKeown, 2001). To help develop language skills with children's literature, provide preschool children with books that represent varied types of language. Some children's books feature the sounds of language; they aid auditory discrimination or incorporate additional phonemes into a child's language repertoire. Others help develop syntactic complexity by using adjectives and adverbs, such as in the book *Swimmy* (Lionni, 1963). Craft books require children to use receptive language by following directions, and wordless books encourage them to create their own stories from the pictures. Concept books feature words such as *up, down, in, out, near,* and *far* or involve children in mathematical reasoning and nonfiction texts offer new concepts and information. When children hear and discuss the language of books, they internalize what they hear and the language becomes their own. Retelling stories read to children encourages them to use book language and incorporate it into their own. Retelling is not an easy task for young children, so props can be helpful, including puppets, felt boards and felt characters, and the pictures in the book. Tape recording a retelling and transcribing it to analyze provides an excellent form of assessment.

The following anecdote recorded by a teacher illustrates how a child incorporated into her language the vocabulary of a book that was read to her and the teacher was able to assess this event.

• • • • • • • • • • • • • • •

While Mrs. Rosen's class is playing on the playground, some birds are circling around. Melissa runs up to Mrs. Rosen and says, "Look, Mrs. Rosen, the birds are fluttering and flapping around the playground." Melissa's descriptive and sophisticated choice of words comes directly from a storybook Mrs. Rosen recently read to the children, *Jenny's Hat* (Keats, 1966). In the book, birds flutter and flap around

Jenny's hat. Melissa had internalized the language of the book and was using it in her own vocabulary, as demonstrated to the teacher.

• • • • • • • • • • • • • • •

There are additional, more focused activities that can be used to enhance oral language development and provide further assessment data, including creating stories, retelling stories, and creating "Very Own Words" word lists from studying a theme. If the theme is healthy foods, ask the children to name their favorite healthy foods. The word list might include *apples, oranges, chicken, cereal, carrots, milk, bananas,* or *bread.* Have real food available and discuss how it looks, smells, feels, and tastes. List the words on a thin long chart and hang it in your room. When you get to the next unit, start a new word list and use the old list to begin a class word list book.

"Very Own Words" can be selected from discussions, art lessons, science experiments, songs, books, poems, cooking experiences, or a theme. The child's name is a popular "Very Own Words" as well. After a particular experience, ask children to name a favorite word. Record children's Very Own Words 5 × 8 cards and store them in their own file box. Have them copy their words and read them. A picture of the word can be on the card as well. Have them read their words and write them as well as a form of assessment.

Helping English-Language Learners in Your Classroom

English-language learners (ELLs) are an important concern. The number of children with different languages grows in our classrooms daily. There are children who do not speak any English and there are children with very limited English proficiency. The English proficiency of the latter group of youngsters varies. The goal is for them to become truly bilingual—that is, equally proficient in English and the home language.

Children also come to school speaking different dialects. A dialect is an alternative form of one particular language used in different cultural, regional, or social groups (Leu & Kinzer, 1991). These differences can be so significant that an individual from a region with one English dialect may have difficulty understanding someone from another region. Dialects are not inherently superior to one another; however, one dialect typically emerges as the standard for a given language. Teachers must be aware of different dialects and help youngsters with the comprehension of standard dialects.

There are general strategies that will support the first language of students in regular classrooms. It is helpful when there is someone in the school who speaks the ELL's first language (Shore, 2001). It could be a child or adult in the school who can speak the home language of an ELL to provide translation. The following strategies expose children in the class to other languages, thus creating an interest and appreciation for different backgrounds:

- Include print in the classroom that is from children's first language.
- Suggest that ELL students share stories in their first language.
- Be sure that children from different language backgrounds have the opportunity to read and see writing with others who speak their language, such as parents, aides, and other children in the school (Freeman & Freeman, 1993).
- Along with the support of children's first language, it is also important to support the learning of English. Assign an English-speaking child as a buddy for the ELL. The Language Experience Approach provides the following types of activities that are helpful for ELLs:
  - Allow children to talk.
  - Have routine story times.
  - Provide thematic instruction that elicits talk, reading and writing, and heightens interests in exciting topics.
  - Write charts based on talk about children's home life and experiences in school.
  - Encourage children to copy experience charts, have them dictate their ideas for you to write, and encourage them to write themselves (Lindfors, 1989; Miramontes, Nadeau, & Commins, 1997).

In the learning environment described throughout this chapter, language development is spontaneous and encouraged. Modeling, scaffolding, and reinforcement make this environment interactive between child and adult, and they guide and nurture language development. The strategies discussed are appropriate for children who have language differences. Some youngsters, however, may need additional attention on a one-to-one basis from the classroom teacher or a resource room teacher (Burns, Snow, & Griffin, 1999; Dickinson & Tabors, 2001). As learning takes place, so does routine and frequent assessment so that learning can be directed toward needs.

PROFESSIONAL DEVELOPMENT

It is recommended that teachers learn how to use the assessments in this chapter. Select several to try with children for their portfolios. Review several standardized tests to see which ones you believe best suit the children in your classroom. Observe and record language during play. Audio record a child speaking a few times during the year, transcribe the samples, and check for t-unit length.

CHAPTER 5

Assessing Phonological Awareness and Early Phonics

• • • • • • • • • • • • • •

Sitting in the doctor's office waiting room, 4-year-old Briar begins to read her sister's diaper bag, which has been labeled with her name. Briar begins to chant her baby sister's name: "Bree, Bree, Avonlee." She repeats the phrase, this time adding, "Would you like to play with me?" Briar smiles and proudly announces to her mom, "Now that's a rhyme!" Her mom smiles in response and Briar in turn begins another chant, "Bbbbrrrriar and Bbbbrrrree, sitting in a tree, happy, happy as can be." Briar turns to the waiting room patients and announces, "Am I good or what?"

• • • • • • • • • • • • • •

B riar's chants are a demonstration of phonological awareness, or the capacity to deal explicitly and segmentally with sound units smaller than a syllable. Awareness at the level of the **phoneme** has particular significance for the acquisition of reading because of its role in the development of the **alphabetic principle** (Liberman, Shankweiler, & Liberman, 1989; Stanovich, 1993/1994). Although Briar has an implicit knowledge of the sounds of her language, to become a fluent reader and writer, Briar—and every child—needs to develop an explicit understanding of the alphabetic principle; that is, they need to know the following:

- Sentences are composed of individual words.
- Words are composed of combinations of individual letters.
- Letters have a predictable relationship with phonemes (phonics).

In this chapter, you will be introduced to informal and formal ways of assessing phonological awareness and early phonics skills. With songs and rhymes and playful activities, teachers can assess children's knowledge and record this information to better inform their instruction. More formal measures will also be discussed and need to be used as well. The vignettes, assessment tools, and methods provided can help you guide your instruction for your students' individual needs.

Defining Phonemic Awareness and Phonics

Phonemes are the smallest sounds in spoken words, and they affect a word's meaning. For example, changing or substituting the first phoneme in the word *cat* from /c/ to /h/ changes the word from *cat to hat* which, of course, changes the word's meaning. **Phonemic awareness** is the ability to notice, think about, and work with the individual sounds in spoken words. Like Briar, most children usually demonstrate their understanding of phonemic awareness informally and in playful situations. They play with the sounds of their language by using alliteration, (as in "Big Bird's brown banana bread and butter") experimenting with rhyming words ("ants in my pants"), and hyperarticulating words ("Bbbbrrrrriar" and "Bbbbbrrrrree").

> Most children usually demonstrate their understanding of phonemic awareness informally and in playful situations.

However, this informal knowledge is often insufficient to translate into conventional reading without direct instruction. The purpose of phonemic awareness instruction is to help children learn to hear and intentionally manipulate these sounds consistently and effortlessly (Cunningham, 1990).

Teachers should also be aware that although phonemic awareness is a widely used term in reading, it is often misunderstood. Phonemic awareness is *not* phonics. Phonemic awareness is the understanding that the sounds of *spoken* language work together to make words. Phonics, on the other hand, refers to the predictable relation between phonemes and graphemes, the letters that represent those sounds in *written* language (Armbruster, Lehr, & Osborn, 2001; Hatcher, Hulme, & Ellis, 1994).

Research Support for Teaching and Assessing Phonemic Awareness and Early Phonics

Over the past decade there has been increasing consensus about what factors contribute to reading success and failure. Reviews by Hurford et al. (1993), Mann (1993), and the National Reading Panel (National Institute of Child Health and Human Development [NICHD], 2000) have noted that a child's ability to hear and manipulate phonemes appears to be a factor that discriminates good readers from poor readers.

The National Reading Panel's report (NICHD, 2000) strongly recommends that, whenever possible, phonemic awareness instruction also be connected to alphabet recognition because this combination appears to further enhance alphabetic understanding. In other words, a child's ability to easily recognize the smallest units of speech and quickly and consistently connect them with their symbolic representations (i.e., letters) allows that child to develop reading fluency (Stanovich, 1986). Longitudinal research has consistently demonstrated that children in programs that use both sound and symbol instruction demonstrate greater improvement in reading than those exposed to a solely oral phonemic awareness program.

Clearly, both phonemic awareness and phonics instruction play important roles in helping children become fluent readers; however, acquisition of these skills is not guaranteed simply through maturation. In fact, about one third of students require varying degrees of assistance to promote development (Adams, 1990). Hence, it is important to consider the best way to introduce and teach phonemic awareness and phonics. Yopp (1992) suggests the following recommendations for teaching these skills:

- Keep a sense of playfulness and fun; avoid drill and rote memorization.
- Use group settings that encourage interaction among children.
- Encourage children's curiosity about language and their experimentation with it.

We also think these recommendations are appropriate for assessing children's understanding of phonemic awareness and early phonics knowledge. With an additional caution, it is important to remember the length of young children's attention spans, so it is better to spend only a few minutes, several times each day engaging preschool children in activities that emphasize the sounds and symbols of language. A few minutes, several times a day maintains the children's interest and enthusiasm yet still provides the necessary repetition without the feeling of being drilled (Vukelich et al., 2007). The following phonemic awareness strategies: rhymes, onset and rimes, sound/symbol isolation and manipulation (beginning phonics) can be taught and assessed using environmental print, songs, poems, and children's literature, as the meaningful context (Yopp, 1992).

> A few minutes, several times a day maintains the children's interest and enthusiasm yet still provides the necessary repetition without the feeling of being drilled.

There appears to be a general developmental sequence that is most successful in helping children develop their phonemic awareness skills,

Table 1
Developmental Progression of Phonemic Awareness

Most Simple	Intermediate	Most Challenging
Hearing rhymes	Segmenting words	Segmenting Sounds
Seeing rhymes	• Syllables	• Initial-ending sounds
Hearing alliteration	Segmenting sounds	Phoneme/Letter Manipulation
Seeing alliteration	• Onset-rime	• Deleting phonemes/letters
	• Initial blending	• Adding phonemes/letters
		• Substituting phonemes/letters

starting with the simplest, e.g., hearing alliteration and rhymes, to segmenting of words in sentences to word segmentation to syllables and onset and rime, to ultimately advancing to blending phonemes and sound manipulation (Bryant, MacLean, Bradley, & Crossland, 1990), as illustrated in Table 1.

So how do preschool teachers appropriately teach and assess phonemic awareness and early phonics? In this chapter we will provide a series of vignettes illustrating how preschool teachers use simple, developmentally appropriate instructional strategies and assessment procedures that both document student growth and refine further instruction. To accomplish this task, teachers use the following:

- Minilessons that target specific skills
- Game-like activities to reinforce instruction
- Multiple, brief (5- to 10-minute) practice sessions
- Focused data collection
- Data to guide further instruction

Teaching and Assessing Rhyme

There is considerable evidence indicating that sensitivity to rhyme makes both a direct and indirect contribution to reading (Mann, 1993; Yopp, 1992). Directly, it helps children appreciate that words that share common sounds usually share common letter sequences. Indirectly, the child's subsequent sensitivity to common letter sequences then makes a significant contribution to reading development. The following scenario offers an example of how Mrs. Foley teaches her young students about rhymes and she assesses their understanding and progress by using a simple teacher-made checklist.

· · · · · · · · · · · · · ·

To help her preschool students hear and see rhymes, Mrs. Foley uses familiar children's songs, poems, and even jump-rope chants. Each week she selects a short rhyme to focus on during opening circle time. During the week she will use the same poem to teach rhymes, letters, and sight words. Today, early in September, she teaches the poem "This Little Bear" to the whole class. Mrs. Foley presents the poem to the children on an enlarged laminated chart and uses a shared reading approach to read the poem (pointing to the words as she reads them). She focuses her minilesson on the skill she intends to assess throughout the week.

> This Little Bear
>
> This little bear has a soft fur coat.
> This little bear rides in a boat,
> This little bear likes to tattle and scold,
> This little bear likes to do what he is told,
> This little bear likes bacon and honey,
> But he can't buy them he has no money.

After they read the poem together two or three times, Mrs. Foley asks the children to reread the poem in pairs and see if they hear any words that sound alike. One pair thinks *coat* and *boat* sound alike. The rest of the class agrees. Another pair thinks *scold* and *told* sound alike. And a small group of children have heard the rhyme of *honey* and *money*. Again, the rest of the class nods in agreement and repeat the rhymes. Mrs. Foley reminds the children that words that sound alike are called rhyming words.

The following day, working with the children in small groups during center time, Mrs. Foley has 4 to 6 children in her group do a choral rereading of the "This Little Bear." She asks the children, "Do you remember what we call words that sound alike?" The children respond, "Rhyme." She now focuses their attention on the pairs of rhyming words, which she has printed on 3 × 5 index cards. She mixes up the word cards and then places them on the table and asks the children to begin to find the matching rhyming pairs. After a few moments, the children realize that the words can be easily matched by looking at the letters at the end of the words. She now brings out another set of rhyming cards, shuffles the cards and places the cards face down on the table and the children begin to play concentration. As the children play the game, Mrs. Foley watches and makes notations on how they respond to both hearing and "seeing" rhymes.

During the week, as the children rotate from center to center, Mrs. Foley continues to teach and collect information about her students' growing understanding of rhyming words and written rimes. At the end of the week she reviews her completed data sheet (see Figure 9).

Figure 9
Assessment of Students' Understanding of Rhyming and Rimes

Week of: November 2
Poem/Song: This Little Bear
Key: 3 = hears all three rhymes   0 = is not able to hear rhyme
Key: 3 = easily sees the written rime   0 = has difficulty seeing the rime

Name	Hears Rhyming Words	Recognizes Written Rime
Barry	3	3
Sheila	3	2
Tory	2	2
Jacob	2	3
Maria	3	3
Megan	3	2
Brent	3	2
Maggie	2	3
Steven B.	2	3
Steven R.	2	3
James	1	2
Angel	1	1
Darlene	2	2
Jessica	3	3
Celina	2	3

As Mrs. Foley reviews the students' progress she confirms her knowledge that a majority of her students can identify rhymes. Likewise, they are learning how to focus their attention on letters within the words and identify rimes (sometimes called word families or patterns). Next, she compared their progress over time by contrasting the results of this assessment with an identical rhyming/rime activity-assessment she completed with the children about a month ago (see Figure 10). As Mrs. Foley reviews their scores she is pleased with the growth she sees for a majority of her students, but she is concerned about James and Angel. This assessment will cause

Figure 10
Growth Over Time

Column 1: Oct. 1
Column 2: Nov. 4
Key: 3 = hears all three rhymes   0 = is not able to hear rhyme
Key: 3 = easily sees the written rime   0 = has difficulty seeing the rime

Name	Hears Rhyming Words		Recognizes Written Rime	
Barry	2	3	2	3
Sheila	3	3	1	2
Tory	2	2	2	2
Jacob	3	2	3	3
Maria	3	3	3	3
Megan	2	3	2	2
Brent	2	3	1	2
Maggie	1	2	2	3
Steven B.	1	2	2	3
Steven R.	1	2	2	3
James	0	1	1	2
Angel	0	1	0	1
Darlene	2	2	2	2
Jessica	3	3	3	3
Celina	2	2	2	3

Mrs. Foley to differentiate her instruction—next week she will have her aide work with them individually on hearing and seeing rhymes and then reassess. If the children don't improve with more instruction she will need to have the regional health services conduct a hearing test.

Since Mrs. Foley has focused lessons on rhyming words over several reading sessions, she offers the students many opportunities to practice hearing rhymes and also gives them a chance to see the letters/word families that make the rhyme. This, in turn, begins to build toward the next step of learning to read.

· · · · · · · · · · · · · · ·

Teaching and Assessing Word Segmentation

Most early phonological awareness activities are taught in the absence of print, but there is increasing evidence that early print activities, using word cards, pointing to print, even spelling words appear to promote phonemic awareness and early phonics (Ehri, 1998). It may be that during spelling and writing activities children begin to combine their phonological sensitivity and print knowledge and apply them to building words. The following vignette demonstrates how Ms. Mills helps her students learn about word segmentation, from hearing words in sentences to the beginning of syllabication of the segments of sound within a word.

· · · · · · · · · · · · · ·

Early in phonological awareness instruction, Ms. Mills teaches her children to segment sentences into individual words. Today, using one of the children's favorite songs, "Row, Row, Row Your Boat," she asks the children to sing the song and clap their hands for each of the words as she points. Next, Ms. Mills continues her efforts to help children find the sound segments within words by taking roll in a special way.

Teacher: Holding Alex's name card, Ms. Mills asks the class whose name is this and they shout Alex! She asks, Is Al-ex here? [claps twice to indicate the number of syllables heard in Alex's name]

Class:	Al-ex [The class responds with two claps. Alex waves hi.]

It takes just a few minutes to take attendance using name-card recognition and syllable-clap, but it is an excellent opportunity to reinforce the children's word knowledge and their ability to hear syllables. This is a ritual the children practice almost daily, but to add to the challenge Ms. Mills also uses vocabulary words that are part of her weekly/monthly science or social studies units. To encourage word recognition she has written the words on sentence strips and has placed them on the "All About Plants" word wall.

Teacher:	Today we are going to continue to learn about growing seeds. What are some of the plant words we learned yesterday?
Sally:	*Seed Coat!* [points to the word *seed coat* that is on the easel]
Teacher:	Yes, Sally can you clap the syllables you hear in *seed coat*? [Sally claps] That's right, *seed* has one clap and *coat* has one clap. Let's all clap *seed coat*. Can you all think of another word?
Nathan:	*Flower* and... [gets up to point to the word on the easel]
Teacher:	Good, Tony, can you clap the sounds you hear? *Flow-er*. [Tony claps]

To assess the children's ability to hear syllables, Ms. Mills relies on observational data. Each week this requires Ms. Mills to predetermine what she will assess. She then creates a simple checklist of the target skills to document her observations. She prints this information out on 2 x 4 labels (see Figure 11). To collect this data, Ms. Mills focuses on several children each day, typically observing a grouping of children sitting together in close proximity; the checklist also helps Ms. Mills keep track of who to observe. This week she is focusing on clapping syllables, name recognition, and unit word recognition.

At the end of the week, the labels are peeled and placed in each child's folder. This helps Ms. Mills document each student's

Figure 11
Weekly Observation Checklist

Martine A. Week: 9/20	Sally J. Week: 9/20
❑ Claps syllables accurately	❑ Claps syllables accurately
✓ Recognizes names	❑ Recognizes names
✓ Recognizes target words (plants/seeds)	❑ Recognizes target words (plants/seeds)
Needs help with hearing word boundaries.	
Tony C. Week: 9/20	**Barbie K.** Week: 9/20
❑ Claps syllables accurately	❑ Claps syllables accurately
❑ Recognizes names	❑ Recognizes names
❑ Recognizes target words (plants/seeds)	❑ Recognizes target words (plants/seeds)
Debbie F. Week: 9/20	**Alex F.** Week: 9/20
❑ Claps syllables accurately	✓ Claps syllables accurately
❑ Recognizes names	✓ Recognizes names
❑ Recognizes target words (plants/seeds)	✓ Recognizes target words (plants/seeds
	Great improvement since August.

progress over time (for example, see Alex's Progress Chart in Figure 12). Alex's chart demonstrates that he is quickly gaining word recognition skills (his classmates' names and targeted unit words), and hearing syllables within the word.

• • • • • • • • • • • • •

Teaching and Assessing Blending and Phoneme Manipulation Through Onset and Rime

Segmenting **onsets** and **rimes**, sometime referred to as word families or word patterns, is the next step in segmenting. An onset is the initial consonant sound(s) of a syllable (e.g., the onset of *cat* is /c/; *stop*, /st/), and the part of the syllable that contains the vowel and all that follows is called the rime (e.g., the letters *at* in *cat*, *hat*, and *sat*, *op* in *stop*). The following vignette describes how Ms. Tower builds the children's word knowledge by beginning with a phonemic awareness activity (hearing rhymes) to sound segmentation (onset and rimes) to initial phonics instruction (letter sound manipulation). Once again this teacher keeps the children engaged and interested by using playful activities for short periods of time (Yopp, 1992).

Figure 12
Alex's Progress Chart

Alex F. Week: 8/21
☐ Claps syllables accurately
✓ Recognizes names
☐ Recognizes target words (Color words)
Recognizes his name and Sally's name.

Alex F. Week: 9/20
✓ Claps syllables accurately
✓ Recognizes names
✓ Recognizes target words (plants/seeds)
Great improvement since August. Recognizes almost every classmate's name.

Likewise, Ms. Tower assesses while she teaches by diligently documenting the children's actions during these playful activities.

• • • • • • • • • • • • •

By January, Ms. Tower's pre-K students are quickly becoming familiar with letter sounds and symbols. In addition to phoneme/letter segmentation activities, she has been reading dozens of books that feature rhymes. Today, during story time, she introduces her students to word families (rimes and onsets). She begins by reading one of her students' favorite books, *Jake Baked the Cake* (Hennesy, 1990). She asks the students to identify some of the rhyming words they hear. Of course, the first words the children list are *Jake*, *bake*, and *cake*.

Ms. Tower isolates the *ake* rime and writes it on the white board. She asks the children to say the word family /ake/ with her. She asks the children what would happen if she added the sound /m/ to the word family. The children and Ms. Tower use "snail talk" to slowly stretch out the sounds to blend /m/ with *ake*. She writes the new word, *make*, on the board. Next, she asks the children to consider what would happen if they added the sound /t/ to the rime. This time, they blend the sounds /t/ and *ake*. Then, Ms. Tower adds the word *take* to the list and congratulates the children on their efforts.

The following day, Ms. Tower asks the children to work in pairs, and she gives each pair a set of magnetic letters and a magnetic board (actually a small, inexpensive cookie pan). She asks the children to look at the list of words they read yesterday. The children quickly read the words that Ms. Tower has placed on the *ake* family word wall. The word wall is a interactive bulletin board that displays words that the children are learning to recognize.

67

Jake	baked
cake	make
take	rake

Ms. Tower asks the children to work together to make one of the /ake/ family words using the magnetic letters. She circulates among the children to see if they are able to make the words. After the children make their /ake/ words, she asks them to share with the group what word they have made. Next, Ms. Tower asks the children to think of what letters would make up the word *rake*. The children quickly start to make the /r/ sound, and they begin to hunt for the magnetic letter *r*. Ms. Tower asks the children to check one another's work as she writes the word *rake* on the /ake/ family word wall. She repeats this process with several other onsets. Some of the words the children create are nonsense words, but she praises the children for listening carefully to the sounds that make up the "word."

During the weeks that follow, Ms. Tower uses a similar procedure to begin to introduce the 37 most common rimes and some of the 500 words they make up. She only uses this exercise, which the children call the Make a Word Game, for about 10 minutes each day. The feeling of fun this game engenders is critical to the children's sense of excitement and contributes to their accomplishments.

Once again, Ms. Tower, like the other teachers we have highlighted, uses a teacher-made checklist list to track the children's progress over time (see Figure 13).

As she reviews her students' progress, Ms. Tower sees great improvement with this skill over time. Initially, she was somewhat concerned that this might be too difficult a skill for her 4-year-olds, but she quickly found that they were learning new letters and word families through these simple phonics activities. The magnetic letters were now becoming one of the hottest games in the Alpha Land center!

• • • • • • • • • • • • • • • •

Obviously children's recognition of onsets and rimes is an important step forward and connects phonemic awareness to phonetic instruction. After a certain amount of sounding-out of letters in words, children come to recognize rimes as familiar spelling patterns. At that point, they can

Figure 13
Tracking Students' Progress With Rimes and Word Families

Key
N = number of words made   M = Sound Manipulation
3 = manipulates sounds easily
2 = beginning to manipulate sound
1 = struggles with sound manipulation

Name	-at 9/9/08		-an 9/20/08		-am 10/9/08		-ake 11/1/08	
	N	M	N	M	N	M	N	M
Jeff	1	1	2	1	3	3	5	3
Rachel	2	1	3	3	4	3	5	3
Sandra	1	2	2	2	3	2	5	3
Bobby	2	2	3	3	4	3	6	3

recognize them without sounding them out (see Figure 14). Figure 14 is meant to help children add onsets at the beginning of the rime and blend them together into a word (e.g., putting the onset *b* at the beginning of the rime *ag* to blend together and make the word *bag*). This quick recognition of rimes therefore is a natural consequence of sounding out letters in words. Children's identification of rimes as such helps them read more rapidly (Snider, 1995).

Teaching and Assessing Sound–Letter Isolation

Although there are 26 letters in the English language, there are approximately 40 phonemes, or sound units. Hence, one of the first goals of phonemic awareness is to help children hear the distinct sounds of the letters. The following vignette demonstrates how Ms. Martin, a preschool teacher uses the children's current interests and prior knowledge to begin a sound isolations activity.

• • • • • • • • • • • • •

"I can read this," says nearly 4-year-old Robbie as he holds up a colorful paper plate. "It says 'Batman.'" I got it at a birthday party yesterday." Ms. Martin responds, "Yes, Robbie. It says 'Batman.'"

Figure 14
Rimes

_ag	_all	_am	_an	_ap	_ar	_at	_ay	_ake	_ad
_ed	_ell	_en	_er	_et					
_id	_ill	_im	_in	_ir	_it				
_og	_op	_or	_ow	_oy					
_ub	_ug	_ur	_ut						

Ms. Martin is always amazed at her preschoolers' abilities to recognize the print in their environment. To capitalize on their prior knowledge and help them learn to hear initial sounds, Ms. Martin has created an Environmental Print "I Can Read" Chart. There already are about 30 logos on the board chart, and the children bring in new objects or wrappers daily. Ms. Martin says the word, "Bbbbbatman," and as she pronounces the word, she hyper-articulates the initial sound. She asks the children to say it with her.

The following day, in the few minutes before the children leave for home, Ms. Martin plays a phonemic/letter awareness reinforcement game that is similar to Hot or Cold, where the students use the volume of their voices to indicate that a student is close to or far from the hidden object. She takes the Batman plate off the chart and sends Remy outside. When Remy is outside, she hides the plate behind the large wooden clock in the front of the room. As she brings Remy inside, her classmates begin to quietly chant /bbb/. As Remy moves toward the front of the room, the other preschoolers begin to increase the volume at which they say /bbb/. Taking her cues from the volume of the chants, Remy turns left. Suddenly, the volume drops to a whisper, so he knows she has gone astray. Turning around, she spots the target. As she quickly moves to pick up the Batman plate, the children yell /BBB/.

Ms. Martin's intentional use of the Environmental Print "I Can Read" Chart helps teach and reinforce the children's knowledge of print and the initial letters and sounds words make. This activity also draws on the students' current interests in and prior knowledge of the print in their homes and neighborhoods (Enz, Gerard, Han, & Prior, 2008). Similar to the chart, in just a few minutes a day, the Hot or Cold game provides the needed repetition to learn a new skill—sound isolation—but without boring or stressful drill.

To help document her students' ability to isolate and discriminate initial letter sounds, Ms. Martin plays a Sound Sort game. She uses 4-by-5-inch drawings or pictures of common objects. Today, she is focusing on the letter sound /b/. She shows the children four pictures and asks them to tell her what each picture is. As the children respond, Ms. Martin repeats what they say, but she elaborates and sustains the initial sound, for example, b-b-b-bed. She tells the children that she needs them to be sound detectives. They need to find the picture that does not start with the /b/ sound. After the children correctly identify the cat, she adds new pictures, some that start with /b/ and some that have different initial sounds. A playful approach to hearing and then discriminating sounds allows children to develop this critical skill with little risk of failure. The children play sound sort for several minutes each day. To document the children's ability to discriminate and isolate sounds Ms. Martin uses a quick worksheet (see Figure 15). She asks the children to circle the objects that start with the letter sound /b/. She collects the worksheets and dates them and puts them in each child's portfolio. This activity is an extension of the game the children are used to playing, so Ms. Martin can assess

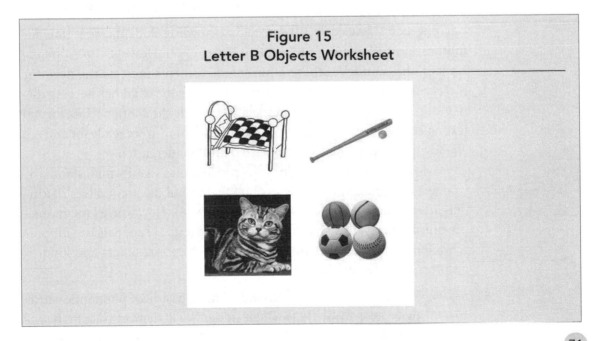

Figure 15
Letter B Objects Worksheet

the children's growing skills and abilities while the children complete the worksheet—thus eliminating the need to conduct more formal tests.

• • • • • • • • • • • • • •

Standardized Assessments for Phonological Awareness and Early Phonics

Developmentally appropriate, highly engaging and playful activities that feature explicit instructional activities, like the ones that are featured in this chapter, are most effective means for teaching young children to hear discrete phonemes. Assessment of these skills at the preschool level serves the following purposes:

- To regularly monitor the progress of students who are receiving instruction in phonological awareness
- To allow teachers to assess the instructional approaches being used and refine them as necessary
- To initially identify students who appear to be at risk for difficulty in acquiring beginning reading skills

At the preschool level, we strongly recommend informal, teacher-designed assessments for a majority of the children. In most cases, these ongoing assessments detect the need for providing students more time for maturation and appropriate, explicit instruction. However, in some instances, the findings of these informal assessments indicate the need for further formal evaluation to determine whether the child has hearing difficulties, language delay, or even specific learning disabilities. More formal testing can be used with those preschool children who are ready for and are already doing work that is not expected until kindergarten.

Most researchers and educators recommend that formal, standardized tests for phonemic awareness not begin until the second half of kindergarten (Chard, Simmons, & Kameenui, 1998). However, as mentioned previously, there will be incidents when these tests are appropriate for preschoolers. When using standardized tests with preschoolers and kindergartners, include the following.

- *Test of Phonological Awareness:* This measure of phonemic sensitivity strongly predicts which students will demonstrate high segmenting ability following small-group instruction in phonemic awareness. The measure consists of one form with 10 items requiring students to indicate which of 3 words (represented by pictures) have the same first sound as a target word and 10 items that require students to indicate which of 4 words (represented by pictures) begins with a different first sound than the other 3. The measure is administered to small groups of 6 to 10 children, is untimed, and students receive raw scores that are normed.

- *Yopp-Singer Test of Phoneme Segmentation*: This test consists of 22 items and requires students to separately articulate each phoneme in the presented words. The student receives credit only if all sounds in a word are presented correctly. If the student gives an incorrect response, the examiner writes the error. Recording the errors helps the teacher decide what remediation the student requires. The student's score is the number of items correctly segmented into individual phonemes. The test is administered individually and requires about 5 to 10 minutes per child.

- *Bruce Test of Phoneme Deletion*: The test assesses phoneme deletion. The measure consists of 30 1- to 3-syllable words. The examiner asks students to delete 1 phoneme from the beginning, middle, or end of a word and to say the word that remains. The positions of deleted phonemes are randomly ordered throughout the test. The test takes about 10 minutes and is individually administered.

- *Auditory Analysis Test*: This measure consists of 40 items arranged in order of difficulty, from deletion of syllables in compound words to deletion of syllables in multi-syllabic words to deletion of phonemes in beginning, middle, and end positions. The teacher asks the student to delete a syllable or phoneme and say the word that is left. The measure is administered individually.

- *DIBELS (Dynamic Indicators of Basic Early Literacy Skills) Rapid Letter Naming*: This test is used to assess the rapid letter naming ability of students. The measure has 18 alternate forms and consists of 104 randomly selected upper and lowercase letters presented on one page. The measure is given individually and students have 1 minute to name as many letters as possible in the order that they appear on the page.

- *DIBELS (Dynamic Indicators of Basic Early Literacy Skills) Phoneme Segmentation Fluency*: This test has 18 alternate forms. Each form consists of 10 words, each with 2 or 3 phonemes, randomly selected from words in the pre-primer and primer levels of the Scribner basal reading series. The timed test is administered individually. Because this measure assesses the number of correct phonemes per minute, it is appropriate for both screening and monitoring progress.

After kindergarten and first-grade teachers review the results of the tests, they have important instructional decisions to make. If students are making slower progress than their average-achieving peers, the teacher can modify instruction; for example, if students are not acquiring segmenting, the teacher may decide to increase the use of more concrete models, such as word cards, magnetic letters, or letter tiles. The teacher may also choose to increase the frequency of instruction in phonemic awareness/phonics throughout the day, or the teacher may work with the parent to make a medical referral to rule out any physical problems (hearing or vision).

Over the past decade there has been increasing consensus about what factors contribute to reading success and failure. Reviews by Hurford et al. (1993), Mann (1993), and the National Reading Panel (NICHD, 2000) have noted that the presence or absence of phonemic awareness appears to be a factor that discriminates good readers from poor readers.

Research indicates that phonological awareness can be taught, it is taught best in combination with letter recognition strategies, and that students who increased their awareness of phonemes facilitated their subsequent reading acquisition (Spector, 1995). This instructional approach ultimately helps children connect letters to sounds, and the decoding process—reading—becomes easier.

PROFESSIONAL DEVELOPMENT

With a study group, create several phonemic awareness activities, from the most basic concepts to the more advanced, that might be used with young children in your classroom. Now develop an assessment checklist to accompany the activity.

With a study group, create several early alphabet recognition activities, from the most basic concepts to the more advanced, that might be used with young children in your classroom. Now develop an assessment checklist to accompany the activity.

CHAPTER 6

Assessing Concepts About Print, Books, and Writing

· · · · · · · · · · · · ·

"Did you put hotdogs on the list?" 3-year-old Robbie asks 4-year-old Lillie.

"No, but I will, just hand me the marker. Ok, there it is," says Lillie. [scribbles and draws a hotdog shape on her "grocery list"] "Ok, what else?"

Thinking, and looking in the kitchen cupboard in the dramatic play center at their preschool, Robbie responds, "Well, we have Trix and Fruit Loops, [reads the labels on the empty boxes] but I think we need Chicken and Stars."

Lillie "writes" down this last request on her grocery list and says, "Now remember, if it's not on the list we can't buy it!"

· · · · · · · · · · · · ·

Lillie and Robbie have learned a lot about print at a very young age. Clearly both children know that print has meaning, language can be written down, and that print is functional and powerful, as illustrated in the preceding vignette. But how did Lillie and Robbie learn these important concepts about print?

This chapter will discuss the assessment of children's knowledge concerning concepts about print, books, and writing. Many assessments that can be performed on a daily basis to keep track of children's achievement, and that will inform your instruction, will be discussed. These assessments are observations of children in different activities and daily performance samples. As you read, think about your own classroom and how the techniques discussed will be applicable for you.

Defining Concepts About Print

Successful beginning readers will develop concepts about print at an early age, even before formal schooling (Goodman, 1986; Harste, Woodward, & Burke, 1984; McGee & Richgels, 1989). They learn these concepts because they have been exposed to print through their own exploration of books that they have access to, or because of parents, grandparents, caregivers, or older siblings who have discussed them. Concepts about print do have to be taught, however, and include the following.

- *Graphic awareness*: An awareness that print carries a message. When children "write" lists and letters or "play read" text using pictures and memory, they demonstrate an understanding of this concept.

- *Writing and its connection to conventions of print*: An understanding that writing is organized in a particular way. Lists start at the top of the page and proceed downward.

- *Emergent reading, concepts about books, and its connection to conventions of print*: An understanding that books are predictable and organized, with a cover, title, and author.

- *Alphabetic principle*: The awareness that printed language consists of sentences, words, and letters. The letters consistently match to the sounds of spoken language (see Chapter 5).

The sections that follow provide ideas and appropriate strategies to teach and assess preschool children's growing knowledge about reading and writing.

Research Support for Teaching and Assessing Concepts About Print and Books

In the early to mid-1900s, educators and parents used strict criteria to define the onset of reading and writing. Children were not considered to be reading until they could recognize numerous printed words, and they were not considered to be writing until they had mastered correct letter formation and could spell words correctly. Children's scribbles and early attempts at reading, such as recognizing store labels, were dismissed as random and irrelevant. By the 1970s, however, some researchers began focusing attention on these initial attempts at reading and writing (Clay, 1975; Read, 1971). The careful observational analysis of children's interactions with print revealed something extremely interesting. Far from meaningless, these early efforts demonstrated a developmental sequence, with the early forms of reading and writing gradually becoming more conventional with age and experience. Further, it also became clear that children's early forms of literacy were not random; instead, these initial efforts were purposeful, thoughtful, and rule-governed (Ferreiro & Teberosky, 1982; Sulzby, Barnhart, & Hieshima, 1989).

This body of research became known as the emergent view of literacy. This perspective significantly changed our understanding of the beginnings of reading and writing. We now know that children begin to learn to read and write by observing adults engaged in reading and writing activities. Over the past quarter century, researchers have documented that most children begin to learn about reading and writing at an early age by observing and engaging in everyday activities with their family and peers (Sulzby, 1985, 1990). By watching their parents write and by having stories read to them, most young children discover patterns and create their own early versions of reading and writing (Morrow, 2009).

While children's early understanding of print begins with their observations of the adults using print in their environment, these observations alone are not sufficient for most children to become proficient readers and writers. Instead, children's early understanding and efforts are an excellent place for teachers to introduce many opportunities to engage with print, such as

- Providing easy access to print, books, and writing materials
- Reading and writing stories aloud
- Demonstrating different types of literacy behaviors (e.g., reading menus, writing notes)
- Answering children's questions about print (e.g., What does this say?)
- Supporting children's literacy efforts (e.g., praising literacy efforts)
- Providing opportunities for children to engage in emergent forms of reading and writing

Further, the most recent research by the National Reading Panel (NICHD, 2000) and our own experiences as parents, grandparents, teachers, and researchers have led us to suggest that preschool children learn about print rather quickly and easily. Thus, preschool teachers should provide more than opportunities to interact with print; they can and should provide appropriate, explicit instruction about concepts about print in preschool.

Teaching and Assessing Children's Graphic Awareness

Using environmental print is an effective way to help develop children's graphic awareness. Environmental print is in school, at home, at the mall, in stores, and all around them, and children begin to recognize logos and branded items. They can read them because they see them a lot and because of the branding. When an adult points out the environmental print, the child's general graphic awareness is heightened. Children begin to recognize environmental print (EP)—print that occurs in real-life contexts—at a very early age. Spiderman, Dora the Explorer, McDonald's, and Goldfish crackers are all examples of insignia that young children recognize—environmental print is everywhere! Many people assume children learn to read when they begin school, but most educators know that literacy development begins long before children reach school age. In fact, observational studies have demonstrated that children as young as 2 are aware of and can read print in their environment (Enz, Gerard, et al., 2008). This type of "reading" involves the child's attention to the whole context (e.g., the picture, color, shape, and even length of the word), rather than just the letters. The logographic is a powerful meaning conveyor; even if children do not recognize the exact word (for instance, saying *Pepsi* for *Coke*), the meaning—soda pop—is directly related (Goodman, 1986).

Children often begin to recognize the letters of the alphabet at about the same time as they "read" environmental print. Interest appears to be a key factor in determining the specific letters that children learn first (McGee & Richgels, 1989). Children's own names and personally relevant environmental print are often the motivation for letter learning.

> Children often begin to recognize the letters of the alphabet at about the same time as they "read" environmental print.

Teachers may use environmental print as a powerful tool to connect children's home literacy to the new literacy activities they are learning at school (Prior & Gerard, 2004; Vukelich et al., 2007). This requires teachers to intentionally draw children's attention to letters that occur in EP. One activity that can be used for this purpose is the EP I Can Read Bulletin Board. With this activity, the teacher asks children to bring from home examples of EP that they can read. Selected pieces are displayed on a bulletin board entitled "I Can Read." For example, the board might contain empty, clean, product containers (cereal boxes, candy wrappers, toy boxes), menus for local fast-food restaurants, shopping bags with store logos, illustrated store coupons, and so on. Children work in small groups to try to figure out the meaning of all the pieces of EP on the board.

Another activity is the EP Alphabet Chart, in which the teacher places pieces of chart paper around the room for every letter of the alphabet. Each day, children bring to class product labels they can "read." During circle time, these labels are read and attached to the correct chart. For example, the Kix (cereal) label would go on the *Kk* page. Then the group reads the labels on all the charts, starting with the *Aa* page.

The following vignette demonstrates how Mrs. Garcia uses her students' knowledge of local fast food restaurants to focus on alphabet letters and sounds.

· · · · · · · · · · · · · · ·

Mrs. Garcia and her preschoolers are singing a song they created about the Pizza Hut restaurant, called the "Pizza Hut Song":

> Pizza Hut, Pizza Hut,
> Kentucky Fried Chicken and Pizza Hut
> McDonald's, McDonald's,
> Kentucky Fried Chicken and Pizza Hut

The children read the laminated songbook as Mrs. Garcia turns the pages. The children love singing and recognizing the colorful logos. Today, after the children sing the song several times, Mrs. Garcia directs their attention to the alphabet letters. "Children, can you find the letter *P*? Araceli, please circle all the letter *P*s you can find!" Araceli uses a transparency pen to circle all the *P*s. "Good job, Araceli!" says Mrs. Garcia. "Boys and girls, what sound does the letter *P* say?" She smiles as all of the children make the /pppp/ sound.

Mrs. Garcia continues for a few minutes more by asking the children to find the *H, K, F, C*, and *M*. As they circle the letters and isolate the letter sounds, she reinforces their efforts.

· · · · · · · · · · · · · · ·

During the week, as Mrs. Garcia works with the children in the Alphabet Center, she asks the children, individually, to identify the letters she names. Because it is essential to assess as we teach, she uses the same Pizza Hut songbook, instructional format and directions as when they were singing with her in a group. Mrs. Garcia used a simple, teacher-made data collection table to track the information for each child. This simple, game-like approach to assessment enables her to sample the letters her young students know and to get a sense of how well her instructional strategies are working. Likewise, she is able to identify students who need extra time and attention to continue to learn the alphabet (Enz, 2005).

Sociodramatic play is another highly effective strategy for incorporating environmental print into the curriculum. As our opening vignette demonstrates, empty product boxes, such as cereal containers, yogurt cartons, and soup cans, can be used in the kitchen area of housekeeping or home centers. As children act out home-related themes, such as making grocery lists or making dinner, they will have opportunities to attempt to read the print on the containers.

To capture this growing knowledge, teachers can make notes, sometimes called teacher reflections (either during or after the event), to add to a child's growth portfolio. In the case of the opening vignette, the teacher would date and make a copy of the reflection for both Robbie's and Lillie's records. This method, described in Chapter 5, is deeply appreciated by parents.

Unlike environmental print that is found in the world outside of school, functional print is typically connected with practical, everyday school activities. Teachers can incorporate functional print by using labels, lists, center management/inventories, schedules, and directions.

For instance, name labels have a wide range of practical classroom uses. Attendance charts can be constructed by placing each child's picture and name above a pocket. The children sign in by finding their name cards in a box and by matching it with their names on the chart. After the children become familiar with their printed names, the pictures can be removed. Likewise, children's names can be used to post on a helper chart. When attendance and helper charts are used on a daily basis, children quickly learn to recognize their own names and the names of their classmates.

Sign-Up Lists or Take Turns Lists are another way teachers can incorporate functional print. Children can write their names on lists to take turns for using a center, toy, playground equipment, or for show and tell.

Initially this is an activity that needs direction from the teacher; however, as children learn to write their name easily and to recognize others' names, they quickly become extremely proficient list managers.

Functional print can also be incorporated through center management and inventories. For example, teachers can encourage cleanup by labeling the places where games need to go when children are finished playing with them. In addition, teachers can ask children to make sure all pieces of the game or prop box are included in their storage box by including a picture/word inventory on the inside of the storage box (see Figure 16).

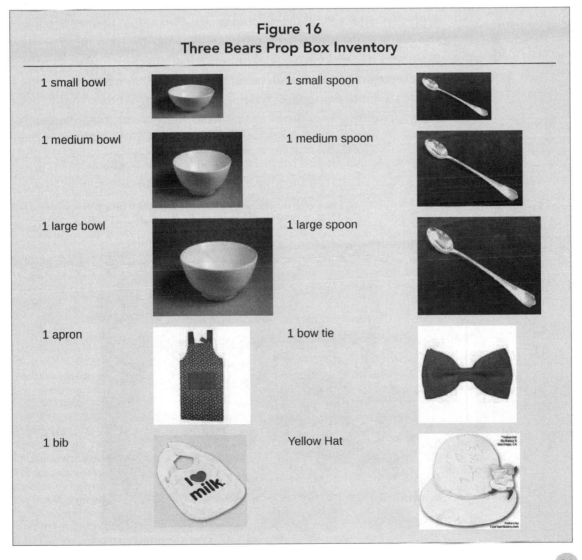

Figure 16
Three Bears Prop Box Inventory

1 small bowl

1 small spoon

1 medium bowl

1 medium spoon

1 large bowl

1 large spoon

1 apron

1 bow tie

1 bib

Yellow Hat

In addition, a daily schedule can be presented at the beginning of class to prepare children for upcoming activities. Pictures can be used to help children remember the different segments of the day. If children ask what is going to happen next, the teacher can help them use the chart to figure it out.

Finally, directions can be posted for taking care of classroom plants or pets or using classroom equipment, such as computers or CD players. Directions can also include recipes for cooking or directions for art activities. Even very young children can follow simple directions that use both words and pictures. At first, children will need help from the teacher in reading these types of directions. Soon, however, they will learn to use the surrounding context to help them remember what the directions say. These activities are what we call functional literacy. Functional literacy behaviors can be captured through observational documentation. Many teachers now take pictures of children engaged in functional activities and then write a brief description of when and what the child did. For example, having a photo of students engaged in writing lists, labeling a block building, or writing a letter to a friend will reveal their engagement, level of achievement, and social and emotional involvement in the activity (see Figure 17).

Figure 17
Student Engaged in Functional Activity

Teaching and Assessing Children's Writing and Conventions of Print

As children learn to recognize and write their names and the names of their peers, writing becomes a valued skill. In the 1980s, Sulzby's (1990) research with preschoolers found children loosely follow a sequence of growth in the production of writing. Sulzby has identified seven broad categories of early writing: drawing as writing, scribble writing, letter-like units, nonphonetic letter strings, copying from environmental print, invented spelling, and conventional writing. It is important to note that Sulzby believes that these categories do not form a strict developmental hierarchy. While there is a general movement from less mature forms toward conventional forms, children move back and forth across these forms when composing texts, and they often combine several different types in the same composition (Sulzby & Barnhart, 1990). Figure 18 illustrates preschooler Tiffany's growth over three years. As you review her development, you will see that the type of writing she used changed as her purposes changed, and her development flourished with her parents and teacher's modeling and support (Christie, Enz, & Vukelich, 2006). Some suggestions for providing children with opportunities to develop their writing skills and knowledge follow. These suggestions include both indirect and direct instruction.

Indirect instruction includes setting up literacy-enriched play centers (see Chapter 3). These literacy-enriched centers provide students with opportunities to demonstrate and practice what they know about reading and writing. The following vignette illustrates this point.

· · · · · · · · · · · · · · · ·

Four-year-old Tanya is working in the writing center. She has created a list of the items in her backpack. She proudly displays the list to her teacher, Ms. Lydia, who responds, "Tanya, what a great, detailed list. What are you going to use it for?" Tanya replies, "I'm going to make sure I have all my stuff and my brother didn't take anything!"

Ms. Lydia has learned that children's writing is important to them, so she first asks the children's permission to copy their work, then quickly labels their work (name, date) and writes a brief description of the level of written effort on the copy (scribble and letter-stream). She then provides a description of the context (in this case, she writes, "Tanya has made an inventory list to track the contents of

Figure 18
Tiffany's Emergent Writing Progression

Drawing as Writing—Grocery list, eggs, pancakes (drawing), milk, and cat food scribble. Age 3

Scribble Writing—"We need to go to the playground!!!" After a minilesson on punctuation. Age 4

Letter-like Units—After seeing a note written by mom to Nane and Papa. Age 4

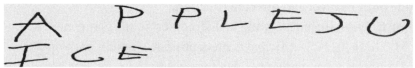

Nonphonetic Letter Strings—Writing the alphabet after instruction in preschool. Age 4½

Copying From Environmental Print—Making a list using the can from the freezer. Age 4½

Invented Spelling—"No pictures in books" Tiffany's note to readers of her book, after teacher modeling during shared writing time. Age 5½

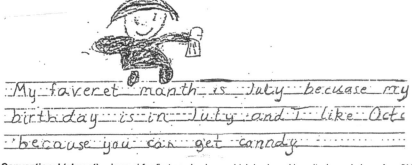

Conventional (almost)—Journal for first-grade class, which is shared in writer's workshop. Age 6½ her backpack"). This work then goes into Tanya's portfolio as evidence of her growing understanding and skill.

Ms. Lydia keeps an ongoing checklist of the data she has collected (see Figure 19). This checklist helps her to manage and focus her data collection over the course of the month. Her goal is to have at least one writing sample, one reading observation, and one **story retell** for each child, each month. Hence, at the end of a semester, she has at least four samples of writing, documented story comprehension checks (see Chapter 7), and reading behavior observations. This data allows her to share information about a child's progress over time. Figure 20 demonstrates how Tanya's knowledge of print has developed over the fall semester. Most impressive is the number of letters she is able to produce. She has obviously been watching her teacher during shared writing time.

Ms. Lydia has found that while the writing center is an excellent place to collect writing samples, the dramatic play center is equally

Figure 19
Writing and Reading Data Collection Inventory

Key
W = Writing sample   S = Story Retell
R = Reading observation   O = Other

Name	Week of Nov. 1	Week of Nov. 8	Week of Nov. 15	Week of Nov. 22
Aaron	W		S	R
Betts	Absent	W	R	S
Candy	R		S	W
Dante	W	R	S	
Elliot		R	W	S
Franco	R	S		W
Gia	S	R	W	
Maria		R	W	S
Nathan	W	S	R	
Opal		S	W	R
Sadie	R	S		W
Tanya	S	Absent	R	W
Vincent	W	R	S	

Figure 20
Tanya's Writing Development

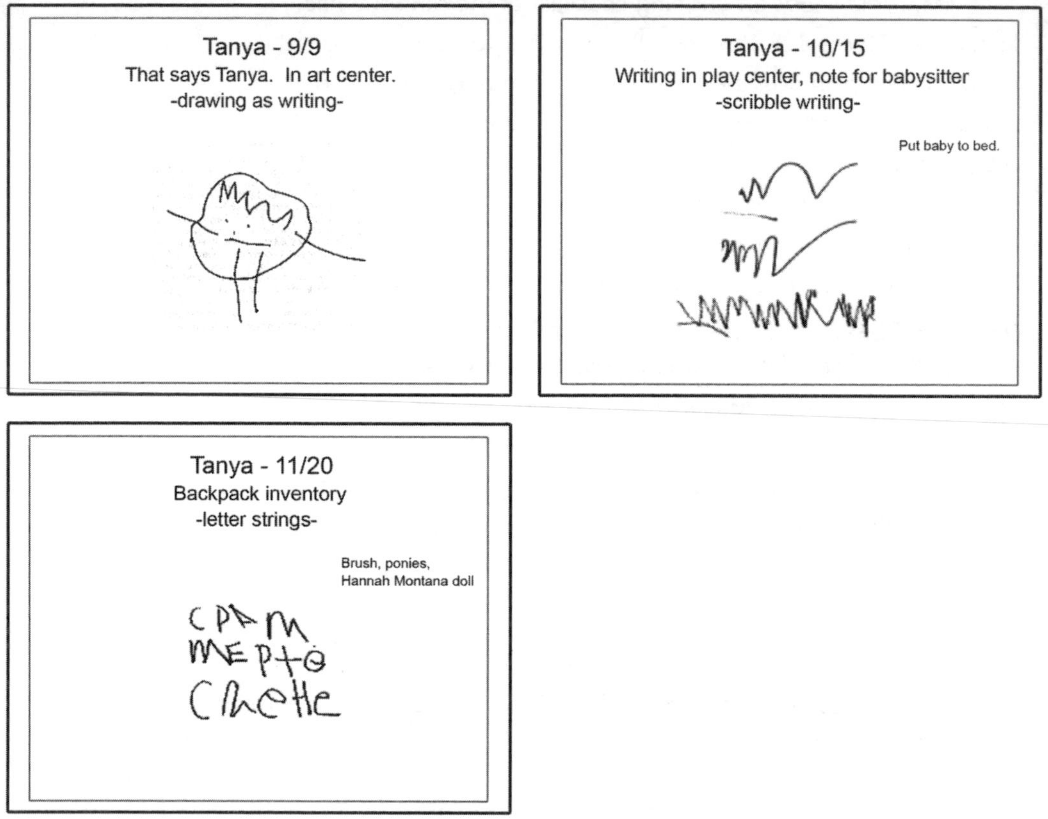

Tanya - 9/9
That says Tanya. In art center.
-drawing as writing-

Tanya - 10/15
Writing in play center, note for babysitter
-scribble writing-

Put baby to bed.

Tanya - 11/20
Backpack inventory
-letter strings-

Brush, ponies,
Hannah Montana doll

CPAM
MEPTO
CAOHE

good. The children write notes, make lists, create tickets and money, and write letters. Likewise, the classroom library is the best place to collect data about how children handle and read books.

• • • • • • • • • • •

Direct writing instruction—oftentimes called shared writing—is an excellent strategy for teachers to use to demonstrate the relationship between speaking, writing, and reading. It can help children realize that (a) what is said can be written down in print and (b) print can be read back as oral language (Allen, 1976; Clay, 1972; Sulzby & Teale, 1987; Veatch, Sawicki, Elliot, Flake, & Blakey, 1979). For very young children, teachers will want to only write two or three sentences at a time. As teachers write they discuss specific aspects about writing through minilessons. As children develop their knowledge about print and attention span, teachers may simultaneously increase the amount of writing and teaching. The following vignette presents a shared writing activity in Ms. Tisha's multi-age preschool classroom in October. The children have been learning about the frog's life cycle, have listened to *The Life Cycle of a Frog* (Wybow, 2002), watched a brief video clip, and then made paper tadpoles.

• • • • • • • • • • • • • • • • •

Teacher: What did we learn about frogs today [in today's final circle time before dismissal]? Turn to your friends and tell them one thing you learned. Remember to listen carefully while they tell you. [Ms. Tisha gives the children two or three minutes to discuss, as this helps her shy children share their thoughts more easily with others.] Ok, who would like to share what their friends said?

Eric: Josh said he learned that tadpoles are baby frogs.

Teacher: How many of you learned that today? [Many heads nod, several hands go up, and some children yell, "ME!"] Would you like me to write that? Raise your hand if you do. [Nearly all of the hands go up.] Ok [she begins to write], tadpoles are baby frogs. Ok, notice I put a space between each word? That way I know where each word begins. What do I put at the end of my sentence?

Children: PERIOD!!!

Teacher: That's right, a period. What else did we learn today? Jeannie, you and Monica are listening so well. What did Monica learn?

Jeannie: Monica said that frogs eat flies and bugs.

Teacher: How many other children learned that frogs eat flies and bugs? [This time everyone raises their hand.] Great, let me write that. Where do I start writing? Jason, can you show me? [Jason points to the left

	hand side of the page.] Great, what do I start with? Karen?
Karen:	A capital, 'cause all sentences start with a capital.
Teacher:	Raise your hand if you agree with Karen. [all hands shoot up] You are all right! All sentences start with a capital letter, and the word *fffffffrogs* [stretching out the sound of the letter *F*] starts with what letter? Who knows the letter?
Children:	F!!!!
Teacher:	Right. [She writes the sentence "Frogs eat flies and bugs."] Ok, let's find out one more thing we learned about frogs today. Jason who was your partner?
Jason:	Terrel. And Terrel said that frogs can lay eggs that hatch in water.
Teacher:	Yes, who else remembered that? [Several children raise their hand.] Let's all read this together. [She begins with the pointer and underlines each word as the children read it. Tomorrow at opening circle she will re-read this story with the children and most likely do a word hunt.] "Tadpoles are baby frogs./ Frogs eat flies and bugs./Frogs lay eggs that hatch in water."

• • • • • • • • • • • • • •

Notice that in this vignette, the shared writing strategy offers children a broad array of learning opportunities; this helps to differentiate instruction for the wide range of skill and knowledge levels represented in this class. At the beginning level, shared writing helps children learn that the purpose of written language is the same as that of oral language: to communicate meaning. For other children, the strategy enables teachers to explicitly demonstrate the structure and conventions of written language. The children watch as the teacher spells words conventionally, leaves spaces between words, uses left-to-right and top-to-bottom sequences, starts sentences and names with capital letters, ends sentences with periods or other terminal punctuation marks, and so on. Shared writing is an ideal means to show children how the mechanical aspects of writing work. Many children learn how to sound out words as they watch the teacher model this strategy when they write. So, this one shared writing activity offered instructional opportunities at many different levels, while reinforcing many skills simultaneously.

Teaching and Assessing Children's Emergent Reading, Concepts About Books, and Conventions of Print

Sulzby (1985) has also investigated the patterns in children's early attempts at reading familiar storybooks. She found that children's storybook-reading behaviors appeared to follow a developmental pattern, with their attention gradually shifting from the pictures to the text and their vocalizations changing from sounding like oral storytelling to sounding like reading. Like the developmental categories of children's writing, this scale does not form a strict hierarchy. While children typically move toward more conventional reading behaviors, they may read in a less mature manner while playing or pretending. The following is a brief list of Sulzby's storybook-reading categories, applied to the "Goldilocks and the Three Bears" story (Sulzby & Barnhart, 1990):

1. *Attending to pictures, not forming stories*: The child looks at the pictures in the book, labeling or making comments about them. (Child: "Bowl, chair, I have a little chair.")

2. *Attending to pictures, forming oral stories*: The child looks at the book's pictures and weaves a story across the pages. However, the child's intonation sounds like he or she is telling an oral story. The listener must be able to see the pictures to follow the story. (Child: "See, she has golden hair and broke the bed.")

3. *Attending to pictures, forming written stories*: The child reads by looking at the book's pictures, and the child's wording and intonation sound like reading. The listener does not usually have to see the pictures to follow the story. (Child: "The three bears went for a walk and then Goldilocks came in the house and saw three bowls of soup. The big bowl was too hot….")

4. *Attending to print*: The child attends to the print rather than to the pictures when attempting to read the story. The child may refuse to read because of **print awareness**, may use only selected

aspects of print (e.g., letter–sound relationships), or may read conventionally.

As children listen to stories during read-aloud time in class, they are carefully observing their teacher handle books and model reading behaviors. Children who have had stories read to them since they were babies have a great deal of knowledge about book and storybook behaviors. Children who have not had this experience will need time and first-hand experience to develop this knowledge.

It is extremely easy to collect information about children's reading behaviors and development. Simply observe children reading to their peers or to the stuffed animals in the classroom library. This information can be entered into a form such as the one pictured in Figure 21. Another way to collect data about a child's reading development is by observing the children (usually in the classroom library) and then documenting the observation through writing anecdotal notes. The class names can be preprinted on 2 × 4 inch labels. The teacher simply needs to add the date and the observed information. This information can then be easily transferred to the child's portfolio (see Figure 22).

Teaching and assessment go hand in hand. As we expose students to experiences we always need to be watching, listening, and taking note of what children have learned and what they still need to know. The following vignette describes Ms. Charles's read-aloud with her 3-year-old preschool students one autumn morning. Notice how she takes a few moments each

Figure 21
Reading Observations

Name	Attending to pictures, not forming stories	Attending to pictures, forming oral stories	Attending to pictures, forming written stories	Attending to print
Belinda		10/3		
Carl		10/3		
Delia			10/10	
Elisha			10/10	
Jeremy		10/18		

time she reads to help her young students learn about the conventions of print and books.

• • • • • • • • • • • • • • •

"The title of the story I'm going to read is *If You Give a Mouse a Cookie* [Numeroff, 1985]." [Ms. Charles holds up a Big Book version of the book and points to the title.] "The print that I am pointing to is called the title of the book and is on the front cover. What do we call this?"

The children respond, "Title!"

"That's right," says Ms. Charles. "It is the title." Then she proceeds to read the story. At the end of the story, Ms. Charles talks to the children about their favorite part of the story, but before she ends story time, she returns to the front cover and asks as she points to the title, "What do we call this part of the book?"

On the following day, as Ms. Charles rereads the story, starting with the title, she asks, "What is this called?" [Several children respond.] "The author of the book is the person who wrote it. The author of *If You Give a Mouse a Cookie* is a lady named Laura Numeroff. I am pointing here where her name is on the cover of the book."

The next day, Ms. Charles asks the children, "Tell me what we call this part of the book?" [pointing to the title]

The children shout, "Title!"

"What do we call the person who writes the book?" asks Ms. Charles. "Yes, we call that person the author. Today, we are going to talk about another special person, the illustrator! The illustrator is the person who draws the pictures in the book. The illustrator of *If You*

Give a Mouse a Cookie is Felicia Bond. I am pointing to her name here on the cover of the book."

· · · · · · · · · · · · · ·

Ms. Charles repeats these little lessons often, knowing that the repetition of such dialogue will help the children to learn these concepts. As the children mature, the conversations can center around more advanced concepts about books. Children need to have adults make this knowledge explicit by labeling and defining these concepts.

Big Books in particular help preschoolers with concepts about books and our assessment of these skills. Big Books are picture storybooks that measure from 14×20 to 24×30 inches. Enlarged print and pictures in these books help children to learn concepts about books, print, and the meaning of text. When using a Big Book, the teacher positions it on a stand so the children can see the pictures and text. As the teacher reads, she tracks the print from left to right across the page and children see where we begin to read on a page. They also learn to differentiate the print from pictures and make the connection that the oral language heard from their teacher is being read from the book. Teachers demonstrate the right way to turn pages with Big Books. We take the top corner of the right-hand page and turn it. The title of the book is prominently displayed on the front of the book, as is the name of the author and illustrator. Children are encouraged to model what the teacher has done by pretending they are reading the Big Book. They do this alone or with a small group of children. They are encouraged to name the author, illustrator, point to the pictures and discuss them, point to the print, turn the pages from the top corner, and so on. This is a perfect time for the teacher to assess behavior in action.

It is important that teachers check students on skills in a one-to-one or small-group setting to really take into account whether they know the skills. Figure 23 is based on Clay's Concepts of Print Test (see Clay, 1975). This assessment is usually completed in stages, with the simplest concepts assessed first (title, author, front and back cover) and then progressing to more complex concepts, such as punctuation marks. It is important to remember that assessment of the children's knowledge must follow the teacher's instruction.

On their way toward reading and writing conventionally, young children construct, test, and perfect hypotheses about written language. Research has shown general developmental sequences with children's early

Figure 23
Concepts About Books and Conventions of Print Checklist

Student's Name _____ Date _____

Directions: The words and phrases in bold are the skills children need to be able to demonstrate. The sentence in italics is the prompt you give a child when assessing his or her knowledge of the conventions of print. This assessment should only be administered after children have had an opportunity to participate in read-alouds where the teacher has labeled the parts of the books and punctuation marks many times. The levels are guidelines that reflect levels of difficulty and may help guide the teacher to the introduction, labeling, and defining of concepts.

Level 1—Concepts About Books

Front Cover: *Show me the front of the book.*
Back Cover: *Show me the back of the book.*
Title: *Show me the title of the book.*
Title Page: *Show me the title page.*
First Page of Text: *Show me the page we read first.*

Level 2—Conventions of Print

Print Carries Message: *Show me where it tells the story.*
Beginning of Text: *Show me where we start to read.*
Left to Right: *Which way do we read the words?*
Top to Bottom: *Which way do the words go from there?*
Return Sweep: *Where do we go at the end of a line?*

Level 3—Concepts About Words and Letters

One-to-One: *Can you point to words as I read?*
Word Boundaries: *Can you put your fingers around a word?*
First Word: *Show me the first word on the page.*
Last Word: *Show me the last word on the page.*
Letter Concept: *Can you put your finger on a letter?*
Capital Letter: *Can you show me a capital letter?*
Lower Case Letter: *Can you show me a lower case letter?*

Level 4—Concepts About Punctuation Marks

Period: *What is this for?*
Question Mark: *What is this for?*
Quotation Mark: *What is this for?*
Comma: *What is this for?*

forms of reading and writing gradually becoming more conventional with age and experience. These early reading and writing forms are known as emergent.

When most children enter preschool they already possess considerable knowledge about reading and writing. Teachers can capitalize on this prior learning by using a number of effective yet simple instructional strategies that link home and school literacy learning.

PROFESSIONAL DEVELOPMENT

Observe several children reading in a classroom library. Observe each child and write an anecdotal note about what the child is doing and what reading level(s) are represented using Sulzby's scale.

Collect children's writing. Describe the context of the artifact. Determine the level (Sulzby's Writing Categories). What does this child know about print? What would be a logical next lesson? Organize this information in the children's portfolios. As you compare their writing over time, what do you notice about the children's knowledge of print?

Observe young children at play in a literacy-enriched dramatic play setting (for example, a home center equipped with paper, pencils, telephone books, television guides, cookbooks, junk mail, cereal boxes, etc.). Watch two or three children while they play in this setting. What do they talk about? What do they write? For example, do they make grocery lists? What does their writing tell you about what they know about the kinds of written language (lists, letter writing, check writing) and forms of written language (scribbles, nonphonetic letter strings, invented spellings)? Do they expect their writing to say something? How do they use the reading materials in the setting? Can they read the cereal boxes? What form of reading do they use to construct meaning from the print? What does your observation tell you about these children's development as readers and writers? If possible, complete this activity with a colleague who watches other children in the play setting. Compare the children's literacy behaviors in the same play setting.

CHAPTER 7

Assessing Children's Comprehension of Text

• • • • • • • • • • • • • •

Ms. Ford and her preschool class take a walk outside on an autumn day to collect leaves. Four-year-old Ethan becomes excited when he finds a cricket. He cups it in his hands yelling, "Come and look!" Everyone gathers to inspect the cricket. Ethan puts the cricket on a rock and the children clap as it hops away.

When they return to the classroom Ms. Ford, taking advantage of this event, thumbs through the bookshelf to find *Quick as a Cricket* (Wood, 1982). She remembers that the cover has a great picture of a cricket and that the book includes many animals and descriptive language ("happy as a lark," "strong as an ox," etc.).

Ms. Ford holds up the book and says, "Look what I found!" Several children see the cover and chant, "A cricket! A cricket!" They gather around Ms. Ford and she begins to read *Quick as a Cricket*. As she reads, Ms. Ford shows the children the illustrations. After reading a few pages, the children get the rhythm of the story ("I'm quick as a cricket, I'm as slow as a snail, I'm as small as an ant"). She reads the page, "I'm gentle as a lamb." She points to the boy in the illustration and says, "He's…" and the children chant the text, "…as gentle as a lamb."

When Ms. Ford and the children finish reading the book, she asks the children which animal they think is most like them and why. Jordon, a very small boy speaks up and says, "I'm strong as an elephant." Natalie then chimes in, "I'm loud as a lion." Ethan says proudly, "I'm quick as a cricket—because I caught a cricket!" When the discussion is over, Ethan whispers to his teacher, "Can I have the book to read?" Ms. Ford is delighted to give Ethan the book.

• • • • • • • • • • • • • •

The experience Ms. Ford provided in this read-aloud afforded her the opportunity to assess children's understanding of and engagement with the experience and the text. Some literal, as well as some interpretive, understanding was required. This activity allowed for teaching and learning. With student input, important assessment information was provided.

The purpose of this chapter is to discuss assessment of comprehension. The strategies and activities that the teacher engages the children in to learn how to comprehend are often the assessment tools as well. These comprehension strategies may simultaneously serve as teaching techniques.

Defining Comprehension

Comprehension is the ability to read or listen to and understand text, which is one of the major goals for reading instruction. Preschoolers are engaged in listening comprehension since they are not conventional readers. Learning to comprehend can begin with young children. It should be an active process when preschoolers listen to stories. Learning to use prior knowledge, children need to interpret and construct meaning about what they listen to (Pressley & Hilden, 2002). When discussion is a part of the experience of reading to a child, adults offer information and children demonstrate what they remember and understand (Teale, 1984).

Research Support for Teaching and Assessing Comprehension

In a study by Durkin (1978/1979), it was found that comprehension was rarely taught in early childhood. Conventional wisdom at the time was, we learn to read in early childhood and we read to learn in the elementary grades. Therefore decoding was taught in the early grades and comprehension beginning in about grade 3. During the 1980s, a great deal of research about comprehension was carried out by the Center for the Study of Reading at the University of Illinois. As a result of that work and other research, more attention has been paid to teaching comprehension to young children. The RAND Reading Study Group report (2002) and the National Reading Panel report (NICHD, 2000) discuss comprehension strategies we need to teach. The comprehension strategies discussed here reflect research and will help children learn to comprehend narrative and expository text.

- Provide background information so that children have some prior knowledge of the text before it is read to them.
- Ask children to anticipate and predict what might happen in a story.
- Read materials to children from beginning to end.
- Have children slow down when they come to information that is relevant to what they want to remember.
- Refer back to the text to clarify some difficult parts.
- Discuss the text with children after reading so they can reflect on ideas and summarize about what was read (Pressley & Afflerbach, 1995).

Comprehension skills are taught from preschool on and throughout our lives. We can begin teaching and assessing the following skills in preschool:

1. Attempts to read storybooks resulting in well-formed stories
2. Participates in story reading by narrating as the teacher reads
3. Retells stories and includes the following elements: (a) setting, (b) theme, (c) plot episodes, (d) resolution
4. Responds to text after listening with literal comments or questions
5. Summarizes what is read
6. Responds to text after listening with interpretive comments or questions
7. Responds to text after listening with critical comments or questions
8. Generates questions that are literal, inferential, and critical
9. Participates in social activities to enhance comprehension, for example, (a) partner reading/buddy reading, (b) visual imagery, (c) discussions, (d) echo reading/choral chanting, (e) tape-assisted reading
10. Recognizes and understands features of expository text, for example, (a) table of contents, (b) glossary, (c) index, (d) charts, (e) descriptive text, (f) text demonstrating a sequence of events, (g) text with a problem that is solved

According to the National Institute of Education, "the single most important activity for building the knowledge required for eventual success in reading is reading aloud to children" (Anderson, Hiebert, Scott, & Wilkinson, 1985, p. 23). Sharing books with children in preschool is associated with increased language complexity, developing comprehension skills, and success in beginning reading (Cosgrove, 1989; Cullinan, 1992; Elley, 1989). When the teacher shares books, children have the opportunity to hear rich and diverse language as well as the rhythm and flow of the words. Read-alouds enrich themes that are explored in the classroom.

> When children are read to, or they read themselves, there should be a purpose for reading or listening.

The good literature that we share with our children will only benefit them if presented in appropriate ways. When children are read to, or they read themselves, there should be a purpose for reading or listening. The format of the **Directed Listening–Thinking Activity** (DLTA) and the **Directed Reading–Thinking Activity** (DRTA) sets a purpose for reading and listening, thus helping to direct thought. This strategy, when internalized by children as a result of frequent use by the teacher, will be transferred and used by students when new material is read or listened to (Morrow, 1984; Stauffer, 1980). For the purposes of this book, we will talk about the DLTA because we are focusing on preschoolers.

A DLTA can have different objectives. The framework, however, is the same: (1) prepare for listening or reading with building background information and setting a purpose for reading, (2) read the story with few interruptions, and (3) after reading, discuss the story based on the objectives. All steps are focused on the DLTA's specific objectives. A DLTA can focus on literal responses (recall of facts, details, etc.) and inferential responses (interpreting characters' feelings, predicting outcomes, etc.). It can focus on identifying story structure elements for narrative or informational text. Research demonstrates that a DLTA and a DRTA can increase the story comprehension of young listeners and young readers (Baumann, 1992; Morrow, 1984; Pearson, Roehler, Dole, & Duffy, 1992).

The strategy provides the listener with a framework for organizing and retrieving information. In the following DLTA for the story *Peter's Chair* (Keats, 1967), the objectives are sequencing the events of the story after it is read and making inferences related to the text.

• • • • • • • • • • • • •

The teacher tells the class, "Today I'm going to read a story entitled *Peter's Chair*. Let's look at the pictures to see if you can tell what the story is going to be about." The teacher encourages the children to discuss the pictures as she turns the pages of the book from beginning to end. She calls this a "book walk." After the children offer their ideas, she says, "This story is about a little boy named Peter whose Mommy and Daddy just brought home a new baby sister. Many of Peter's things, such as his baby toys, high chair, and crib, are being painted pink for his sister. Peter gets upset thinking that his family doesn't love him anymore. Do you have a younger brother or sister? Do you have to share your toys with your little brother or sister? How does that make you feel? Do you have to give them some of your things, such as your crib and high chair? Were you sad or happy about that and why? If you don't have a brother or sister, how does it make you feel to share with friends? When I read the story you will hear about how Peter feels about his new baby sister and having to share his belongings with her. Try to decide if you would feel as Peter does."

· · · · · · · · · · · · · · ·

Students should be prepared for listening with prereading questions and by building background knowledge. Background knowledge related to what is going to be read when introducing a story is crucial. It helps children focus their thinking about the story and aids comprehension. Ask pre-questions that build additional background knowledge and set a purpose for listening. Determine what children know and don't know about the topic. Relate the questions to real-life experiences whenever possible, as in the preceding vignette.

While reading the story, show the children the pictures as you read. Stop just one or two times for comments or questions during the story. Save the discussion for the end, as interrupting for a lot of discussion interferes with comprehension.

The post-reading discussion should be guided by the objectives for listening to the story. This discussion will give you an idea of whether the children listened and understood. For example, some good discussion questions and activities for the previous vignette would be the following:

1. What things that belonged to Peter did his parents prepare first, second, and third for the new baby?

2. What would you have done if you were Peter?

3. Do you think Peter's parents were right to take Peter's things and give them to his baby sister?

4. How would you feel if your parents took your things and gave them to your baby sister or brother if you had one or have one?

Teaching and Assessing Comprehension Through Repeated Storybook Reading

Children enjoy repetition. Being familiar with an experience is comfortable, like singing a well-known song. A repeated story helps develop concepts about words, print, and books. It also increases the number, kind, and complexity of responses. Preschoolers in a **repeated reading** study gave more interpretive responses; they predicted outcomes and made associations, judgments, and elaborative comments (Morrow, 2009). Children also began to narrate stories as the teacher read, focused on elements of print, and asked the names of letters and words. With older children, those who were considered struggling readers also provided more responses with repeated readings than with a single reading (Kuhn & Stahl, 2003; Rasinski, 1990).

> Children who select a book that has been read to them many times are able to read it themselves or participate in pretend reading.

Children who select a book that has been read to them many times are able to read it themselves or participate in pretend reading. Since early storybook experiences should be pleasurable, select texts that children can comprehend. Evaluate the texts to read to young children based on the following:

- The content of the text is familiar.
- Children have some background knowledge required to understand the text.
- Children are interested in the topic.
- The syntactic complexity of the sentences will be understood by the children.
- Most of the vocabulary will be familiar with some new words as well.
- The length of a selection is appropriate (Graves, Juel, & Graves, 1998).

The following dialogue is from a transcription used for assessing word study and comprehension knowledge of a 4-year-old after hearing a story read three times (see Morrow, 1996). Marcy took part in this discussion with sophisticated responses to *The Three Little Pigs* (Brenner, 1973). The excerpt includes the child's comments and questions and the teacher's responses. Most of the story text has been omitted.

• • • • • • • • • • • • •

Teacher: Today I'm going to read the story *The Three Little Pigs*. It is about three pigs who wanted to leave home and build their own houses and take care of themselves. [The teacher begins to read the story. When she gets to the part where the wolf says to the first little pig, "Little pig, little pig, let me come in," Marcy chimes in.]

Marcy: "Not by the hair of my chinny chin chin. Then I'll huff and I'll puff and I'll blow your house down."

Teacher: Very nice, Marcy, you are helping me with the reading. [continues to read]

Marcy: I want to read that part, but I don't know how.

Teacher: Go ahead and try. I bet you can. I'll find the part and help you.

Marcy: [pretend reads parts she remembers from the repeated readings] "The little pig ran to his brother's house; the one that had the house made of sticks."

Teacher: [continues reading] "The wolf got to the pig's house that was made of bricks and said..."

Marcy: [chants with the teacher and points to the words on the page] "'Little pigs, little pigs let me come in,' said the wolf. 'Not by the hair of my chinny chin chin,' said the pigs. 'Then I'll huff and I'll puff and I'll blow your house down,' said the wolf."

Teacher: You're right again, Marcy. [The teacher reads to the end of the story.] Did you want to say anything else about the story?

Marcy: The wolf scared the pigs. But they learned they need to have strong houses. I want to see the part again when the pigs leave home. [Marcy searches through the pages.]

Teacher:	Show me the part you are talking about.
Marcy:	There it is, at the beginning. The pigs are packing their bags and saying good-bye to their mommy and daddy.
Teacher:	How do you think their mommy and daddy felt when they all left home together?
Marcy:	I bet they were sad. I want to look at the part when the wolf falls down the chimney into the pot of boiling water.
Teacher:	Here it is.
Marcy:	The wolf fell, jumped down the chimney and ended up in a pot of boiling water and ran out the door and never came back again.
Teacher:	That's terrific.
Marcy:	That's what the story said.
Teacher:	You're right.

• • • • • • • • • • • • •

This sophisticated response can only happen when a child has heard a story that has been repeated. This discussion tells us a great deal about the child's story comprehension. She knows the sequence of the story. She includes details in her retelling. She also used different voices to depict the characters and inferred meaning based on the pictures and her understanding of what was happening. Several repeated reading discussions should be audio or video recorded to hear progress after one reading, a second, and even a third. There should be a repertoire of books considered favorite stories that are read repeatedly to children.

Teaching and Assessing Comprehension Through Shared Book Experiences

A shared book reading (Holdaway, 1979) is usually carried out in a whole-class setting, although it may be done in small groups. During this activity, teachers model fluent reading. They help to develop listening skills because children are asked to participate in the story reading. This provides an opportunity for assessment since children are active in the story reading and we can see and hear their participation. Participation can include chanting repeated phrases in the story, stopping at predictable parts and asking children to fill in words and phrases, or asking children to read keywords that are special to the story. **Shared book experiences** could also include echo reading, where the teacher reads one line and the children repeat it.

Audio or video record shared book readings and make them available in the listening center. This provides a familiar and fluent model for reading with good phrasing and intonation for children to emulate. A DVD of this experience will tell the teacher a lot about the listening and participation skills of the individual children in the class. Research indicates that shared book reading benefits the acquisition of reading and writing by enhancing background information, sense of story structure, and familiarizes children with the language of books (Cullinan, 1992; Morrow, 1985). Book language is different from oral language. It introduces new syntax and vocabulary, as is found in the following excerpt from the story *Swimmy* (Lionni, 1963): "One bad day a tuna fish fierce swift and very hungry came darting through the waves."

Predictable stories are ideal for shared book experiences because they allow children to guess what will come next. Predictable books use catch phrases and rhymes, such as in *Green Eggs and Ham* (Seuss, 1960). Books and stories with cumulative patterns are predictable, since new events are added with each episode and then repeated in the next, as in the well known story "I Know an Old Lady Who Swallowed a Fly." This story repeats phrases and patterns as it continues. When reading, the teacher looks for the children's participation by having them fill in the repeated phrases and rhyming words she leaves out. The words in brackets are those left out by the teacher for children to fill in.

I know an old lady who [swallowed a fly,]

I don't know why she swallowed a fly, I guess she'll die

I know an old lady who swallowed a spider

That [wiggled and jiggled and tickled inside her]

She swallowed the spider to catch the fly,

I don't know why she swallowed a fly, I guess she'll die

I know an old lady who swallowed a bird,

How absurd to swallow a [bird.]

She swallowed the bird to catch the spider

That [wiggled and jiggled and tickled inside her]

She swallowed the spider to catch the fly

I don't know why she swallowed the fly

Perhaps she'll die.

Other predictable books are those with conversation, such as *Goldilocks and the Three Bears* (Izawa, 1986) or *The Three Billie Goats Gruff* (Brown, 1957). All books become predictable as children become familiar with them, so repeating stories builds a repertoire for shared book experiences. Books that carry familiar sequences, such as days of the week, months of the year, and letters and numbers are predictable, such as Eric Carle's *The Very Hungry Caterpillar* (1969). Teachers can watch children in the group for participation in these shared book experiences or check the child on a one-to-one basis or in a small-group setting.

Teaching and Assessing Comprehension Through Small-Group and One-to-One Story Readings

Reading to small groups and to individuals must not be overlooked. Often considered impractical in school settings, one-to-one and small-group readings yield tremendous benefits because of the interactive behavior it involves, along with the direct information it gives the child. It also provides the adult with insight into what the child already knows and wants to know. Preschoolers do well participating in small-group and one-on-one readings, since they need the attention the setting provides (Morrow, 1988).

When teachers manage small-group storybook reading by initiating interactive discussions, the number and complexity of the children's responses increases. The youngsters will offer many questions and comments that focus on meaning. They label illustrations initially and then give more attention to details. Their comments and questions become interpretive and predictive, and they draw from their own experiences. They also begin narrating—that is, "reading" or mouthing the story along with the teacher. When frequently involved in small-group or one-to-one storybook readings, children begin to focus on structural elements in a story, remarking

---

Figure 24
Story Discussion Guidelines

Teacher Behavior During Storybook Reading

1. Manage
   a. Introduce the story.
   b. Provide background information about the book.
   c. Redirect irrelevant discussion back to the story.

2. Prompt Responses
   a. Invite children to ask questions or comment throughout the story when there are natural places to stop.
   b. Scaffold responses for children to model if no responses are forthcoming.
   c. Relate responses to real-life experiences.
   d. When children do not respond, ask questions that require answers other than yes or no.

3. Support and Inform
   a. Answer questions as they are asked.
   b. React to comments.
   c. Relate your responses to real-life experiences.
   d. Provide positive reinforcement for children's responses.

---

on titles, settings, characters, and story events. After many readings the children begin to focus on print, reading words, and naming letters and sounds (Morrow, 2009). Figure 24 offers a chart to help with prompts during story discussion to promote comprehension.

The following transcriptions assess small-group story readings in preschool. The groups had three children in each. They sat on the floor with the teacher in a little circle and everyone could see the book. The vignettes illustrate the questions and comments children make. They allow us to see the rich information children receive from the teacher and subsequently, the children's rich responses. The transcriptions demonstrate what children comprehend and what they don't understand. This assessment data helps the teacher design instruction.

Book Concepts

In the following vignette, the child demonstrates an interest in concepts about books. Because the group listening to the story is so small, it is possible for the teacher to engage in a conversation with Jerome concerning the questions he has.

• • • • • • • • • • • • • •

Story: *The Very Busy Spider* (Carle, 1985)

Jerome: [pointing to the picture on the front of the book] Why does it have a picture on it?

Teacher: The cover of the book has a picture on it so you will know what the story is about. Look at the picture. Can you tell what the book is about?

Jerome: Ummm, I think that's a spider. Is it about a spider?

Teacher: You're right, very good. The book is about a spider, and the name of the story is *The Very Busy Spider*. When you look at the pictures in a book they help you find out what the words say.

• • • • • • • • • • • • • •

Child Asks for a Definition

After the teacher reads the title of the book, Jovanna, who is used to the small-group readings, feels confident to ask a question and knows the types of questions to ask from past experience, as illustrated in the vignette that follows. In this case, the discussion will enhance her vocabulary.

• • • • • • • • • • • • • •

Story: *Where the Wild Things Are* (Sendak, 1963)

Teacher: I'm going to read a story called *Where the Wild Things Are*.

Jovanna: What are Wild Things?

Teacher: It is a person or an animal that acts angry, or excited, or very active, and maybe a little scary. See, there is a picture of a wild thing in the book.

Jovanna: I never knew that before. They do look scary and angry and excited!

• • • • • • • • • • • • • •

Noticing the Print

In the next vignette, the small-group reading allows the child to be so close to the book and the print that he can really be engaged in noticing print items of interest. He also is secure enough to point out what he has found in the book—that the page is filled with words that begin with the letter *P*.

. . . .

Story: *The Pigs' Picnic* (Kasza, 1988)

Colin: Wait, stop reading. Look at all the *p*s on the page. See, here is one. Here is one. What does that say?

Teacher: This word is *pig*, and this is *picnic*, and this is *perfect*. You are right; they all begin with a *p*.

. . . .

Predictions

In the segment that follows, higher level comprehension is occurring. Dorene is thinking out loud about the story and is wondering what is going to happen. In this case, the prediction has to do with what the birthday present will be.

. . . .

Story: *Mr. Rabbit and the Lovely Present* (Zolotow, 1962)

Dorene: I wonder what the present will be.

Teacher: I don't know. Look at the pictures before I start reading and see if you can get an idea.

Dorene: Well, I see them picking apples, pears, and grapes. Maybe they will give her mother some fruit for her birthday.

Teacher: That is a good thought; let's read the book and find out.

. . . .

Making Text-to-Text Connections

In the following vignette, we see the most sophisticated comprehension occurring. The teacher sets the stage by suggesting that the book has interesting *illustrations*, a word her preschoolers are familiar with because she uses it frequently. As James looks at the illustrations, he is able to make connections between those characters in *Knuffle Bunny* and some things that happen in the *Mary Poppins* DVD he has seen at home.

Story: *Knuffle Bunny* (Willems, 2004)

Teacher: Did you notice the interesting illustrations in *Knuffle Bunny*? They are very interesting.

James: Hey, that is like *Mary Poppins* DVD. In *Mary Poppins* sometimes it is real people who are the characters and sometimes it is pretend with cartoons. In *Knuffle Bunny* it is the same. The background is with real pictures—you know the kind you take with a camera—and the characters are color cartoons.

The children's comments in these vignettes demonstrate literal understanding, interpretive ability, and critical associations—relating the stories to their lives and making predictions and judgments about characters. There are comments about print, such as names of letters, words, and sounds. Although whole-class readings are more practical and have tremendous value in exposing children to literature, the interactive behavior between adult and child in one-to-one readings and small-group readings does not occur in the large-group setting. When reviewing transcripts of story readings in all three settings, we find that in whole-group settings, a child cannot ask questions or comment throughout with so many in the class. In a whole-group setting, the discussion must be managed by the teacher and consequently, he or she says more than the children. In small-group and one-to-one readings, after initial modeling by the teacher, most of the dialogue comes from the children (Morrow, 2009).

Teaching and Assessing Comprehension Through Teacher- and Child-Generated Questions

Productive discussions that yield important information for the teacher to use about what children know and need to learn result from good questions. Discussions must include more than a few words by participants and include questions that ask for clarification, explanations, predictions, and justifications. The following is a list of categories for asking questions.

Literal questions ask students to

- Identify details such as who, what, when, and where
- Classify ideas
- Sequence text
- Find the main idea

Inferential and *critical* questions ask students to

- Provide background knowledge
- Relate text to life experiences
- Predict outcomes (What do you think will happen next?)
- Interpret text (Put yourself in the place of the characters—how would you feel? What would you do?)
- Compare and contrast
- Determine the problem and the solution

Discussion questions should reflect children's interests and have many appropriate responses rather than just one correct answer. Questions should stimulate responses reflecting a child's feelings about what was read to them. These questions ask children to deal with feelings and images. Other questions deal with facts, details, and the main ideas. When asking questions, children can look in the book to find pictures to help answer the questions. Eventually, children should be encouraged to ask their own questions about a story that was read to them.

> Discussion questions should reflect children's interests and have many appropriate responses rather than just one correct answer.

Teaching and Assessing Comprehension Through Story Retelling

Encouraging a listener or reader to retell a story helps develop a child's vocabulary, syntax, comprehension, and sense of story structure (Ritchie, James-Szanton, & Howes, 2003). Retelling engages children in holistic comprehension and organization of thought. It also allows for original thinking as children mesh their own life experiences into their retelling (Gambrell, Pfeiffer, & Wilson, 1985). With practice in retelling, children come to assimilate the concept of narrative or informational text structure. They learn to introduce a narrative story with its beginning, setting, theme, plot episodes, and resolution. They also learn to retell narrative text in their particular structure, such as a sequence structure, cause-and-effect, or problem/solution. In retelling stories, children demonstrate their comprehension of story details and sequence. They also infer and interpret the sounds and expressions of characters' voices. In retelling informational text, children learn to sequence events, describe in detail the information presented, and determine cause and effect.

Retelling is not an easy task for children, but with practice they improve quickly. To help children develop the practice of retelling, let them know before they listen to a story that they will be asked to retell it (Morrow, 1996). Further guidance depends on the teacher's specific purpose for the retelling. If the immediate intent is to teach sequence, for instance, then children are asked to think about what happened first, second, and so on. If the goal is to teach the ability to make inferences from the text, ask the children to think of things that have happened to them that are similar to those that happened in the story. Props, such as felt-board characters or the pictures in the book, can be used to help students retell. Pre- and post-discussion of text helps to improve retelling ability, as does the teacher's modeling a retelling for children.

Retelling is a tool to teach as well as a tool to evaluate children's progress. If you plan to evaluate a retelling, tell the child during your introduction of the selection that he or she will be asked to retell it after the reading. If you are assessing a retelling, do not offer prompts beyond general ones such as "Then what happened?" or "Can you think of anything else about the selection?" Retellings of narrative text can reveal a child's sense of story structure, focusing mostly on literal recall, but they also reflect a child's inferential thinking. To assess the child's retelling for sense of story structure, first divide the events of the story into four categories—setting, theme, plot episodes, and resolution. Use a guide sheet and the outline of the parsed text to record the number of details the child includes within each category in the retelling, regardless of their order. Credit the child for partial recall or for retelling the "gist" of an event (Pellegrini & Galda, 1982). Evaluate the child's sequencing ability by comparing the order of events in the child's retelling with the proper order of setting, theme, plot episodes, and resolution. The analysis indicates the elements the child includes or omits, how well the child sequences, and most important, where instruction should be focused. Comparing analyses of several retellings over time will indicate a child's progress. Some story retelling guidelines are as follows (Morrow, 2009, p. 217):

1. Ask the child to retell the story. "A little while ago, I read the story [name the story]. Would you tell (retell) the story as if you were telling it to a friend who has never heard it before?"

2. Use the following prompts, if needed:

    a. If the child has difficulty beginning the retelling, suggest beginning with "Once upon a time," or "Once there was"

    b. If the child stops retelling before the end of the story, encourage continuation by asking, "What comes next?" or "Then what happened?"

    c. If the child stops retelling and cannot continue with general prompts, ask a question that is relevant to the point in the story at which the child has paused. For example, "What was Jenny's problem in the story?"

3. When a child is unable to retell the story, or if the retelling lacks sequence and detail, prompt the retelling step by step. For example,

    a. "Once upon a time" or "Once there was…"

    b. "Who was the story about?"

    c. "When did the story happen?" (day, night, summer, winter?)

    d. "Where did the story happen?"

    e. "What was (the main character's) problem in the story?"

    f. "How did (he or she) try to solve the problem? What did (he or she) do first (second, next)?"

    g. "How was the problem solved?"

    h. "How did the story end?"

The following example uses an outline of the narrative story *Franklin in the Dark* (Bourgeois, 1987). The outline is accompanied by a transcription of a child's retellings of the story. A retelling guide sheet and a transcription of a story told by a child named Philip follows (see Morrow, 1996).

• • • • • • • • • • • • • •

Story Outline

Setting: Once upon a time there was a turtle named Franklin.

Characters: Franklin (main character), Franklin's Mother, a bird, a duck, a lion, a polar bear.

Theme:	Franklin is afraid to go into his shell since it is dark inside the shell.

Plot Episodes

First episode:	Franklin decided to look for help to solve his problem.
Second episode:	Franklin meets a duck and asks for help. The duck tells Franklin that he wears water wings since he is afraid of the water.
Third episode:	Franklin meets a lion who wears ear muffs since he is afraid of his own roar.
Fourth episode:	Franklin meets a bird who is afraid to fly so he uses a parachute.
Fifth episode:	Franklin meets a polar bear who wears a hat, mittens, and a scarf since he doesn't like the cold.
Sixth episode:	Franklin shares his experiences with his mother.
Resolution:	Franklin and his mother put a nightlight in his shell. Now Franklin will go inside his shell.

Verbatim Transcription (Philip, age 4)

Teacher:	What's the title of the story I read to you today?
Philip:	I don't know.
Teacher:	*Franklin in the Dark*.
Philip:	*Franklin in the Dark*. One time Franklin didn't want to go in his shell. He was too scared. But his Mama says, there's nothing in there. But Franklin didn't want to go in the shell because he thought there was monsters in there. He didn't like to go in because he was scared. It was dark. At the end he went in, he turned on a little night light and went to sleep. That's it.

• • • • • • • • • • • • •

Figure 25
Story Retelling Analysis Form

Setting
__ Begins story with an introduction
__ Names main character
__ List other characters named
__ Includes statement about time and place

Theme
__ Refers to main character's goal or problem to be solved

Plot Episodes
__ Episodes are recalled
__ List episodes recalled

Resolution
__ Includes the solution to the problem or the attainment of the goal
__ Puts an ending on the story

Sequence
__ Story is told in sequential order

Retellings can be evaluated for many different comprehension tasks. The directions for students prior to retelling and the method of analysis should match the goal. Figure 25 provides an analysis form for evaluating a retelling. The teacher checks for the elements a child includes and to determine progress over time.

In his retelling Philip names the main character Franklin and Franklin's mother. Philip does state the problem of the main character or the theme. He does get the resolution of the story and ends it. The parts of the story that Philip included are told in sequential order. In his retelling Philip does not begin the story with an introduction. Aside from mentioning Franklin and his mother, he does not talk about any of the other four characters. There is no statement of time and place. Philip does not recall any of the plot episodes in the story. We know from this evaluation that Philip is able to recall the theme of the story and the resolution. We especially need to work on helping Philip to remember details of a story, such as characters and plot episodes, and also to begin the story with an introduction.

On the other hand, 5-year-old James was able to retell the entire story of the three pigs without leaving anything out. He did use the book as a guide. He told the story in several voices, that is, the voice he created for the wolf, the pigs, and the narrator. He told the story to a rhythm he created. He read some of the words from the text such as *Thump* when the wolf knocked on the door, and *Splash* when he fell into the pot of boiling water. Interestingly he called the boiling water "hot lava" first and then changed it to "boiling water." The class had discussed volcanoes prior to reading the story of the three pigs and his background knowledge was used in this story where it actually made sense. James also said, "When the wolf fell into the pot of boiling water he hurt his butt." This was not the language in the book. We had video taped this segment of James for assessment purposes and it gave us interesting information. Whenever he was having trouble remembering he put his head down, turned his head away from the book, and it was obvious that he was thinking. His body language told us he was uncomfortable. He finished the story and the teacher said, "The End," at which time James said, "No, I didn't sing the song." He was referring to "Who's Afraid of the Big Bad Wolf." He sang the song and as soon as he finished it he said as he shut the book, "The End."

Comprehension Assessment

There are several techniques for assessing students in this chapter. There are taped transcriptions to analyze; there are discussions to record and review. Have one-to-one interviews with children as well as whole-group and small-group sessions to evaluate your students. Ask questions and encourage responses in a whole-group, small-group, or during an individual interaction. Children's comprehension of stories can be demonstrated and evaluated through their retellings, attempted reading of favorite storybooks, role-playing, picture sequencing, use of puppets or felt-boards to re-enact stories, and their questions and comments about stories. Keep periodic performance samples of activities, such as audio or video recordings of retellings.

Throughout this chapter assessment tools for evaluating strategies have been provided. Most of the assessments are daily performance samples made up of transcribed recordings. These materials should be placed in a child's portfolio to evaluate his or her concepts about books and comprehension of text. Baseline data from children should be collected early in the school year with assessment measures repeated a few times a year. Figure 26 provides a checklist of all skills discussed to check how students are doing.

Figure 26
Checklist for Assessing Concepts About Books and Comprehension of Text

Child's Name: _____ Date: _____

	Always	Sometimes	Never	Comments
Concepts About Books				
Knows a book is for reading				
Can identify the front, back, top, and bottom of a book				
Can turn the pages properly				
Knows the difference between the print and the pictures				
Knows that pictures on a page are related to what the print says				
Knows where to begin reading				
Knows what a title is				
Knows what an author is				
Knows what an illustrator is				
Comprehension of Text				
Attempts to read storybooks resulting in well-formed stories				
Participates in story reading by narrating as the teacher reads				
Retells stories and includes the following elements: (a) setting, (b) theme, (c) plot episodes, (d) resolution				
Responds to text after listening with literal comments or questions				

(continued)

Figure 26 *(continued)*

	Always	Sometimes	Never	Comments
Can summarize what is read				
Responds to text after listening with interpretive comments or questions				
Responds to text after listening with critical comments or questions				
Generates questions that are literal, inferential, and critical				
Participates in social activities to enhance comprehension, for example, (a) partner reading/buddy reading, (b) visual imagery, (c) discussions, (d) echo reading/choral chanting, (e) tape-assisted reading				
Recognizes and understands features of expository text: (a) table of contents, (b) glossary, (c) index, (d) charts, (e) descriptive text, (f) text demonstrating a sequence of events, (g) text with a problem that is solved				

Using Standardized Tests to Assess Comprehension

We've discussed standardized tests in other chapters of the book. Preschoolers' comprehension is difficult to measure with standardized tests because children this age aren't usually conventional readers. Listening comprehension is really what is tested at this age. Most standardized tests begin in kindergarten. The Dynamic Indicator of Basic Early Literacy Skills (DIBELS) is a test that is often used with preschoolers—it measures other skills as well as comprehension and is age-appropriate.

The DIBELS test consists of a set of procedures and measures for assessing the acquisition of early literacy skills. The tests are individually administered; they are designed to be short (one minute) fluency measures used to regularly monitor the development of pre-reading and early reading skills. DIBELS are comprised of seven measures to function as indicators of phonemic awareness, alphabetic principle, accuracy and fluency with connected text, reading comprehension, and vocabulary. DIBELS were designed for use in identifying children experiencing difficulty in acquisition of basic early literacy skills to provide support early and prevent the occurrence of later reading difficulties. It is included because it has a measure of comprehension in it that most early literacy tests do not. DIBELS Indicators of Individual Growth and Development for Infants and Toddlers (IGDI's) is a set of measures designed and validated for use by early childhood practitioners and interventionists for the purpose of monitoring children's growth and progress. Unlike standardized tests that are administered infrequently, IGDI's are designed to be used repeatedly by practitioners to estimate each child's "rate of growth" over time. The distinctive benefit of this approach is that the information can be used to directly inform intervention design, implementation, and modification at reasonable levels of training, time, and cost. DIBELS Get it Got it Go! is a test for preschool-aged children. For more information, see www.dibels .org, dibels.uoregon.edu/youngerchildren.php, and www.getgotgo.net.

PROFESSIONAL DEVELOPMENT

As part of the ongoing professional development in this book, teachers can begin a portfolio for some of their children and try the following. Read the same story at three different times to a child. Record the child's question-and-answer session after each reading. Compare the difference in performance.

Ask a child to do a retelling of an expository text. If the structure of the text is descriptive, remind the child about what you are looking for. Tape the retelling and evaluate it.

Ask children to make up questions about who, what, when, and where for a story, then have the child make up questions about how the character felt, or what he or she would do in the character's situation.

CHAPTER 8

Planning, Managing, and Sharing Data

• • • • • • • • • • • • • •

Ms. Evans is reviewing her curriculum requirements for the month of October. As she reviews the monthly curriculum goals established by the Head Start agency, she begins to determine how she is going to focus her weekly instruction. After she drafts the weekly plans, she begins to identify what performance data she needs to collect each week. To help her with this process, she uses the Language and Literacy Standards for Preschool Children. Ms. Evans knows that while the local Head Start agency will formally assess the children during the year, this information does not directly help her know what her children are learning on a day-to-day basis, nor does this information help her to immediately refine her instruction.

• • • • • • • • • • • • • •

Today the demands of accountability for national and state standards and grade-level objectives are foremost in mind for administrators and teachers in both public and privately funded preschools. As we discussed in Chapter 1, nearly every state has articulated what preschool children need to learn. Hence, this in turn prescribes what preschool teachers/administrators need to include in the curriculum.

In the area of language arts and literacy, representatives of the two major literacy organizations, IRA and the National Council of Teachers of English, have worked collaboratively to construct a set of content standards for the United States (1994). Additionally, IRA and NAEYC have jointly issued a position statement on developmentally appropriate reading and writing practices for children (1998) that includes a list of what children of various ages and grade levels can likely do.

While preschool student progress (particularly in federally and state-supported programs) may be measured on standardized tests that occur biannually, effective preschool teachers know they must assess children's progress continually. Ongoing assessment guides instruction and helps students make consistent progress. As the students are introduced to new information, teachers can determine what was clear to students and what needs to be re-taught. Teacher instruction, student learning, and assessment are continuously intertwined activities. This chapter offers practical ways to collect assessment data and measure children's progress.

Determining What to Assess

In this chapter we will observe how Ms. Evans, a veteran Head Start teacher, uses her curriculum and language and literacy goals to develop her monthly goals, weekly lesson plans, and instructional activities. Ms. Evans then uses her weekly curriculum learning activities as opportunities to assess, collect student work called artifacts, and make observations of student interactions. Ms. Evans's comprehensive assessment system

- Allows children multiple ways to reveal their unique abilities and talents
- Presents a total picture of the student's social and intellectual growth
- Is fair and reflective of the local and national norms of student achievement
- Is understandable and respected by parents and administrators

Curriculum Expectations Drive Data Collection

Determining what to assess is a multiple-step process. First, Ms. Evans must consider the curriculum guidelines. Figure 27 reveals the curriculum expectations for this Head Start agency. Ms. Evans has found the monthly overview actually provides an anchor for weekly instruction and assessment (see Figure 28). As Ms. Evans considers how she will present information to the children over the course of each week, she simultaneously considers what language and literacy knowledge preschool children are expected to master in preparation for kindergarten. Figure 29 offers a simple checklist of these expectations. These first three steps guide the curriculum development:

1. Review curriculum goals—monthly curriculum map
2. Develop week-by-week planning guide
3. Determine language and literacy standards for preschool children

Figure 27
Head Start Curriculum Overview Map

Month Theme Character Pillar	Concepts Examples	Objectives	Letters/ Numbers
August/September Self Respect	• Body Awareness • Five Senses • Emotions • Transition from home to school	• The child will understand that he/she is unique and will be strengthened in his/her self-esteem.	4 letters: M, F, A, H 1–5 number recognition (Aug–Dec)
October Our Community Responsibility	• Community Helpers • Fall Harvest	• The child will understand that he/she is part of the larger community.	3 letters: D, P, L
November Families and Neighbors Sharing	• Family Structure • Friendships • 4 food groups	• The child will understand that all families are unique.	3 letters: N, O, B
December Home and Traditions Sharing	• **Cultural Diversity** • Giving	• The child will understand that all families have different traditions.	3 letters: C, W, T
January It's a New Year Fairness	• Winter/Seasons • Calendars • Time	• The child will understand the cycles of time.	3 letters: S, Q, U numbers 6–10 (Jan–May)
February Healthy Living Citizenship	• Nutrition • Dental • Hygiene • Exercise	• The child will learn the importance of taking care of his/her body.	3 letters: V, X, E
March Life Cycles Caring	• Domestic/Wild • Insects • Plants	• The child will become familiar with a variety of animals and the cycles of living things.	3 letters: Z, Y, K
April Our Earth Trustworthiness	• Caring for the Earth • Earth History (dinosaurs) • Spring • Begin transition activities	• The child will understand his/her relationship to the Earth.	4 letters: J, I, G, R
May/June Safety Review all pillars	• Sun Safety • Tricky people • Water Safety • Complete transition	• The child will develop safety awareness.	Review all letters and numbers

Note. Adapted from the Western Arizona Council of Governments—Head Start Agency.

Figure 28
Week-by-Week Planning–October

Week Theme Character Pillar	Content	Concepts	Letters/ Numbers
Week 1 Growing Things Taking care of our mini gardens	• Parts of seeds • Plant life cycle • Conditions for plant growth	• Target vocabulary • Sequencing growth cycle • Sorting and categorizing seeds	Target letters P, L Review F 1–5
Week 2 Growing Things Taking care of our mini gardens	• Identifying vegetables • Comparing plant growth	• Target vocabulary • Review five sense vocabulary • Hearing syllables	Target letters D Review P, L, F 1–5
Week 3 Community Helpers Job responsibilities	• Grocer, farmer, doctor, dentist, bus driver, teacher, police, and fire	• Who does what type of work? • Review emotion vocabulary	Target letters D Review P, L, F, A, H 1–5
Week 4 Growing Things Taking care of our mini gardens	• Identifying vegetables • Comparing plant growth	• Target vocabulary • Sequencing growth cycle • Sorting and categorizing seeds • Comparative language	Review P, L, F, A, H, D 1–5

Figure 29
Language and Literacy Standards for Preschool Children

Listening Comprehension
__ Listens with increased attention
__ Understands simple oral directions
__ Listens to and engages in conversation

Speech Production and Discrimination
__ Identifies differences between similar sounding words
__ Produces speech sounds with increased ease and accuracy
__ Experiments with language

Vocabulary
__ Shows an increase in listening and speaking vocabulary
__ Uses new vocabulary in daily communication
__ Refines understanding of words
__ Increases listening vocabulary

Phonological Awareness
__ Begins to identify rhymes
__ Begins to attend to beginning sounds
__ Begins to break words into syllables or claps with each syllable
__ Begins to create words by substituting one sound for another

(continued)

Figure 29 (continued)

Verbal Expression
__ Uses language for a variety of purposes
__ Uses sentences of increasing length, grammatical complexity
__ Uses language to express routines
__ Tells a simple personal narrative
__ Asks questions
__ Begins to retell stories in sequence

Print and Book Awareness
__ Understands that reading/writing are ways to obtain information
__ Understands that reading/writing communicates thoughts/ideas
__ Understands that illustrations carry meaning but cannot be read
__ Understands that letters are different from numbers
__ Understands that a book has a title and an author
__ Understands that print runs from left to right and top to bottom
__ Begins to understand basic print conventions

Letter Knowledge and Early Word Recognition
__ Begins to associate letter names with their shapes
__ Identifies 10 or more printed letters
__ Begins to notice beginning letters in familiar words
__ Begins to make some letter sound matches
__ Begins to identify some high-frequency words

Motivation to Read
__ Demonstrates an interest in books and reading
__ Enjoys listening to and discussing books
__ Requests being read to and re-reading the same story
__ Attempts to read and write

Knowledge of Literary Forms
__ Predicts what will happen next in a story
__ Imitates special language in a book
__ Asks questions about the information/events in a book
__ Connects information and events in books to real life

Written Expression
__ Attempts to write messages
__ Uses letters to represent written language
__ Attempts to connect the sounds in a word with their letter forms
__ Begins to dictate words/phrases for an adult to record on paper

Data Collection Drives Instruction

Understanding curriculum goals and learning standards helps to determine instructional activities, which then offers opportunities for developing data collection tools. These tools allow Ms. Evans the ability to assess students' growth and progress as they engage in learning activities. The assessments then help Ms. Evans to reflect upon her instruction in terms of the students' learning. If the assessment demonstrates the children are learning, she can proceed to introduce new skills and information, but if the assessments indicate that students are not learning the intended content, then Ms. Evans must reconsider how and what she is teaching. These next three steps help Ms. Evans assess students and her instruction:

4. Design weekly learning activities
5. Align activity assessment tools
6. Confirm/refine instruction

Ultimately, all of these efforts are synthesized into a teacher's ability to document and describe an individual child's growth and development over time. Ms. Evans uses a portfolio system that includes samples of student work, anecdotal and observation notes, and formal and informal assessment measures. All this information will be shared with parents to enable them to easily see their child's development. For instance, Figure 18 in Chapter 6 demonstrates Tiffany's development over a three-year period (see page 84), while Figure 20 in Chapter 6 shows a student's growth over a few months (see page 86).

Finally, this information can also be aggregated (summarized across all students) and shared with other audiences, such as government officials or building administrators, for a variety of reasons, including federal reporting, administrative accounting, and curriculum purchases.

Ms. Evans begins her planning by consulting the Curriculum Overview Map in Figure 27. This is her first step in determining curriculum goals and instructional activities. To guide weekly planning, Ms. Evans next expands upon the content and specific concepts the children need to learn. At this point, Ms. Evans begins to consider specific learning activities. As she writes the week-by-week planning guide she also consults Figure 29 to determine specific skill development beyond the letters and numbers. She realizes that the growing plants lessons will offer the children many opportunities to develop language and literacy skills. She quickly highlights the skills she intends to focus on during this month. It is for these highlighted skills that Ms. Evans will develop informal assessments that will help her to quickly determine and document how well the children are learning.

Now Ms. Evans begins to plan her learning activities, again combining the curriculum goals for the Head Start program and the language and literacy standards for preschool children. As she plans her activities she

Figure 30

October Week 1 Lesson Plan and Assessment Overview

Month: October   **Theme:** Community Helpers and Fall Harvest—Plants
Letters: D, P, L   **Numbers:** 1–5   **Character Pillar:** Responsibility
Content: The child will understand that he/she is part of the larger community.

Week 1: Growing Things	• Parts of seeds • Plant life cycle • Conditions for plant growth	• Target vocabulary • Sequencing growth cycle • Sorting and categorizing seeds	Taking care of our mini gardens
Week 2: Growing Things	• Identifying vegetables • Comparing plant growth	• Target vocabulary • Review five-sense vocabulary • Hearing syllables	Taking care of our mini gardens
Week 3: Community Helpers	• Grocer, farmer, doctor, dentist, bus driver, teacher, police, fire	• Who does what type of work? • Review emotion vocabulary	Job responsibilities
Week 4: Growing Things	• Identifying vegetables • Comparing plant growth	• Target vocabulary • Sequencing growth cycle • Sorting and categorizing seeds • Comparative language	Taking care of our mini gardens

simultaneously considers how she can collect data about how the children are learning new information. Figure 30 provides an example of her planning. The highlighted components illustrate the activities and skills that she intends to employ to collect student performance data.

Children will require a couple of weeks of repetition to develop new vocabulary and knowledge, yet some children will demonstrate high levels of skill rather rapidly. By collecting information on this checklist over the course of the month, Ms. Evans can continue to refine her instruction and confirm every child's growing skill.

Assess as You Teach

Ms. Evans develops learning activities that both teach content and specific skills and directly reflect her unit assessment. For example, during group time that begins the school day, Ms. Evans introduces the song "The Plants Begin to Grow," which is sung to the tune of "The Farmer in the Dell." This song also helps to introduce the discussion about conditions for growing plants, which includes planting the seeds in soil, then applying water and sun. She also uses this song to introduce target words to place on the word wall. As they practice singing the song each day, Ms. Evans identifies two or three children to carefully observe. At the beginning of the unit she often assesses the children who are more confident, then each week adds more children.

Through the week, after the children sing the song (as she points to the words), Ms. Evans stops and asks the children to find specific words by showing the children word cards, such as those shown in Figure 31. The children then try to find the words in the song. She calls upon two or three children at each session and records their word recognition/matching on the Plant Unit Assessment Checklist (see Figure 32).

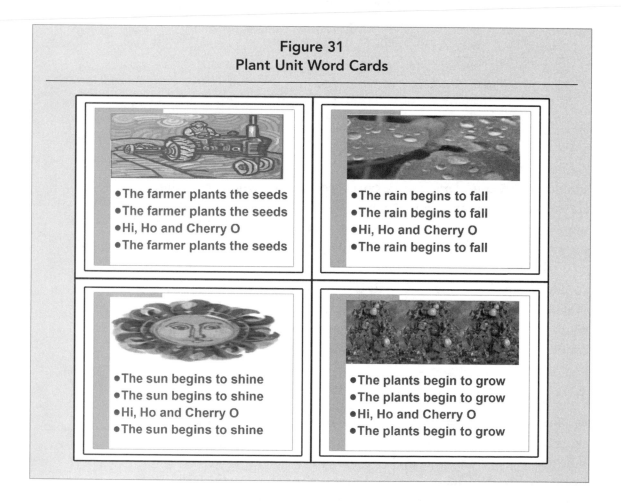

Figure 31
Plant Unit Word Cards

- The farmer plants the seeds
- The farmer plants the seeds
- Hi, Ho and Cherry O
- The farmer plants the seeds

- The rain begins to fall
- The rain begins to fall
- Hi, Ho and Cherry O
- The rain begins to fall

- The sun begins to shine
- The sun begins to shine
- Hi, Ho and Cherry O
- The sun begins to shine

- The plants begin to grow
- The plants begin to grow
- Hi, Ho and Cherry O
- The plants begin to grow

Figure 32
Plant Unit Assessment Checklist

To be used during small-group activity or observations of group activity during play—Ms. Evans simply circles the correct response or the words the child recognizes.

Child's Name	Recognizes Words	Hears Syllables	Identifies Plant Parts	Explains Plant Cycle	Uses Target Vocabulary	Recognizes Symbol/Sounds		
						D	P	L
	Plant Seed Sun Rain	Y N	plant, seed, root, stem, leaf, flower	Y N	peas, beans, squash, spinach, lettuce, broccoli, carrot, radish cauliflower, watermelon, sunflower	Symbol Y N Sound Y N	Symbol Y N Sound Y N	Symbol Y N Sound Y N
	Plant Seed Sun Rain	Y N	plant, seed, root, stem, leaf, flower	Y N	peas, beans, squash, spinach, lettuce, broccoli, carrot, radish cauliflower, watermelon, sunflower	Symbol Y N Sound Y N	Symbol Y N Sound Y N	Symbol Y N Sound Y N
	Plant Seed Sun Rain	Y N	plant, seed, root, stem, leaf, flower	Y N	peas, beans, squash, spinach, lettuce, broccoli, carrot, radish cauliflower, watermelon, sunflower	Symbol Y N Sound Y N	Symbol Y N Sound Y N	Symbol Y N Sound Y N
	Plant Seed Sun Rain	Y N	plant, seed, root, stem, leaf, flower	Y N	peas, beans, squash, spinach, lettuce, broccoli, carrot, radish cauliflower, watermelon, sunflower	Symbol Y N Sound Y N	Symbol Y N Sound Y N	Symbol Y N Sound Y N

Figure 33
Vegetable Word Cards

As Ms. Evans progresses to story time she reads the story *The Surprise Garden* (Hall, 1998). The story is about a family who plants a number of "mystery" seeds and then watches what happens as the garden blooms and bears produce. To enhance the children's vocabulary she has created vegetable cards that show the seeds and/or plant of the vegetables that were grown in the story (see Figure 33). As she introduces the vegetables, she shows the cards she has created (in PowerPoint format using information found on the Internet). After the story the class will "play" with words, talking about the first letter and sound, placing the cards on the word wall and clapping the syllables. Once again, Ms. Evans and her aide observe the children and identify what children know and can do. This information is then documented on the Plant Unit Assessment Checklist in Figure 32. Using the checklist and targeting a few specific students each day helps Ms. Evans evaluate her instruction as well.

Portfolio Management System

After Ms. Evans collects information during the week, she then begins the process of maintaining a portfolio for each child. A portfolio allows the teacher to document a student's progress over time and share that information with parents, other teachers, and administrators. Ms. Evans has found that the portfolio management system allows her to collect and analyze samples of her children's work, anecdotal notes, and vignettes, and also include formal tests such as the ones the Head Start agency requires, and informal assessment measures, such as her checklists.

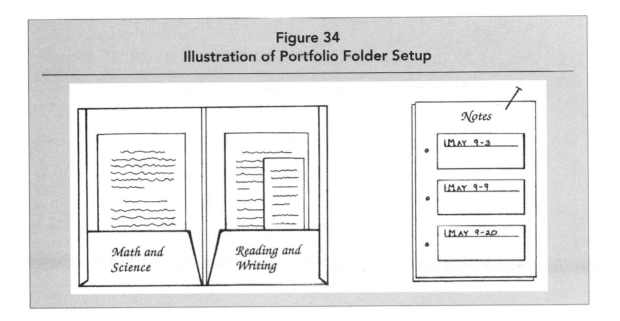

Figure 34
Illustration of Portfolio Folder Setup

How Are the Assessment Measures and Products Stored?

Ms. Evans, like many teachers, finds that folders with pockets and center clasps for three-hole-punched paper serve as excellent portfolios (see Figure 34). When anecdotal notes and vignettes are written on computer mailing labels, the labels can be attached to the inside covers of each student's folder (Enz, Kortman, & Honaker, 2008). When these notes are written on index cards, the cards can be stored in one of the folder's pockets. Also, a sandwich bag might be stapled inside each student's folder to hold an audiotape or CDs. The self-sealing feature of the bag means that the tape can be securely held inside the folder. The class folders might be housed in a plastic container with hanging files.

What Information Should Teachers Collect?

Typically, products or work samples (sometimes called artifacts) demonstrate children's literacy knowledge and skill in performing an authentic, real-world literacy task. The children might write a grocery list or create a sign or write a food order. Each of these products is different and may display a different level of writing. Writing samples collected over the course of a year will demonstrate how the child's use of writing develops. Each sample should have an explanation of the context, the date, the child's

Robbie 9/9

- In the hardware store (dramatic play center)

- List of supplies to buy—hammer, saw, nails

name, and a brief statement about what the effort reflected (NAEYC & National Association of Early Childhood Specialists in State Departments of Education, 2004), as in the example in Figure 35.

Products. Robbie's sample is a photocopy, but photos may also be used to demonstrate work samples; for example, 3-year-old Darlene created signs for the Pizza Hut dramatic play restaurant. The signs included a wall menu that was very detailed and too large to fit into her folder. The teacher took a picture of the sign and then made a note on a 2 × 4 inch label that she attached to the back of the picture when she printed it out. Pieces placed in the portfolio are selected because they show children's everyday performance related to the language and literacy standards.

Checklists. As mentioned earlier in this chapter, the teacher's weekly learning activities should drive the data collection opportunities. These predetermined and developed skill-related assessments usually include whole-group checklists, such as the checklist in Figure 32, or individual assessment checklists (see Chapter 6, Figure 23, on page 93). Group check-lists can be copied and included in individual folders. Teachers should take care to black out other students' names when sharing this type of data with parents.

Observation Notes. Certain centers, such as the library center or the dramatic play center, provide rich opportunities to collect anecdotal or ob-servation notes. The teacher or classroom aide will want to try to system-atically collect observational data by using 2 × 4 inch labels with the children's names preprinted on the label (for an example see Figure 21 in Chapter 6). To keep the portfolios updated, Ms. Evans takes time each week to place artifacts, observation notes, and completed checklists in the students' files. This time also helps her to organize the data collection she will need to conduct the following week. Keeping track of children's sam-ples is one way to help the teacher know what to collect and from whom.

Sharing Student Progress With Parents, Administrators, and State/Federal Agencies

Sharing Progress With Parents

The success of the parent–teacher relationship depends on the teacher's ability to highlight the child's academic and social strengths and progress. Parent–teacher interactions reach their full potential when parents and teachers share information about the child from their unique perspectives, value the child's individual needs and strengths, and work together for the benefit of the child (Vukelich et al., 2007). When areas of concern are dis-cussed, it is important to provide examples of the child's work or review the observational data to illustrate the point. It is also essential to solicit the parents' views and suggestions for helping the child and to provide con-crete examples about how they might help the child learn. Whenever pos-sible, connect these concerns to your views, as this reinforces the feeling that the teacher and the parents have the same goals for helping the child learn.

Ms. Evans uses the children's portfolios during parent–teacher con-ferences where the child's social/emotional development and academic progress are discussed. Ms. Evans has found that these conferences help her learn more about each child's home environment, while giving parents a chance to learn about their children's progress in the school setting.

During the conference, Ms. Evans shares information about each child's academic growth by reviewing the contents of the portfolio and discussing the preschool learning standards she is teaching (see Figure 29 on pages 122–123). As she shares the information on the checklists, she briefly describes how each of these skills helps the child to become a reader and writer. The following is a brief portion of a parent–teacher conference in which Ms. Evans discusses the conventions of print checklist and how these behaviors contribute to reading.

• • • • • • • • • • • • • •

Ms. Evans: Let's review Emily's knowledge about books and print. [shows parents the Conventions About Print Checklist for Emily, provided in Figure 36] This checklist is used four times a year to see what the children know about books and what I still need to teach them. You can see that Emily has a great deal of early understanding about books.

Mom: What can I do to help Emily?

Ms. Evans: We will be learning more about words. Reading to Emily and actually pointing to the words as you read is very helpful for young readers to learn that each written word equals one spoken word.

Mom: When I was a kid, they wouldn't let us point to the words.

Ms. Evans: It was that way for me too, but now teachers know that pointing to the words is actually a good thing for young children. [proceeds to share Emily's writing samples as shown in Figure 37]

• • • • • • • • • • • • • •

Many times Ms. Evans has found that parents do not recognize their child's scribbles as the beginning of reading and writing, so she takes time to discuss how these early efforts are part of a developmental sequence. To help discuss how Emily is actually using her writing to accomplish tasks she sees adults completing, Ms. Evans shows Emily's mom her writing samples. She uses a chart similar to Figure 18 in Chapter 6 (see page 84). The following is a summary of this discussion.

Figure 36
Conventions of Print Checklist for Emily

Student's Name __Emily__

Directions: The words and phrases in bold are the skills children need to be able to demonstrate. The sentence in italics is the prompt you ask a child when assessing his or her knowledge of the conventions of print. This assessment should only be administered after children have had an opportunity to participate in read-alouds where the teacher has labeled the parts of the books and punctuation marks many times. The levels are guidelines that reflect levels of difficulty and may help guide the teacher to the introduction, labeling, and defining of concepts.

Date	Conventions of Print Checklist

Level 1 October 15

Y N **Front Cover:** *Show me the front of the book.*
Y N **Back Cover:** *Show me the back of the book.*
Y N **Title:** *Show me the title of the book.*
Y N **Title Page:** *Show me the title page.*
Y N **First Page of Text:** *Show me the page we read first.*

Level 2 December

Y N **Print Carries Message:** *Show me where it tells the story.*
Y N **Beginning of Text:** *Show me where we start to read.*
Y N **Left to Right:** *Which way do we read the words?*
Y N **Top to Bottom:** *Which way do the words go from there?*
Y N **Return Sweep:** *Where do we go at the end of a line?*

Level 3

Y N **One-to-One:** *Can you point to words as I read?*
Y N **Word Boundaries:** *Can you put your fingers around a word?*
Y N **First Word:** *Show me the first word on the page.*
Y N **Last Word:** *Show me the last word on the page.*
Y N **Letter Concept:** *Can you put your finger on a letter?*

Level 4

Y N **Capital Letter:** *Can you show me a capital letter?*
Y N **Lower Case Letter:** *Can you show me a lower case letter?*
Y N **Period:** *What is this for?*
Y N **Question Mark:** *What is this for?*
Y N **Quotation Mark:** *What is this for?*

Figure 37
Emily's Writing Sample

Emily   9/15
Home center
- Grocery List—donuts, eggs, bacon, pizza
  -drawing as writing-

Emily   10/20
Restaurant center
- Taking an order
  -scribble writing-

Emily   11/01
Writing center
- Making a book
  -scribble writing with some letter like units-

Emily   11/30
Writing center
- Writing address
  -letter like units (notice the numbers)-

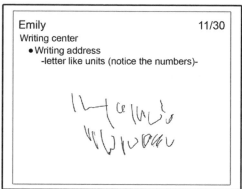

• • • • • • • • • • • • •

Ms. Evans: Let's review Emily's writing development. As you can see she is using print knowledge to write a really good grocery list. Her drawings are the first step towards using "writing" to communicate.

Mom: Oh my gosh! Her drawings look like what she wants to get! These are some of her favorite foods.

Ms. Evans: Notice how she is using scribble writing? Notice how much her scribble writing looks like adult cursive writing? Now look at this sample. She is writing a book and notice how she is writing from left-to-right and from top-to-bottom? She has even filled the whole page just like the books she sees in our classroom.

Mom: I had never noticed how much she is watching adult writing.

Evans: Now look at her address. We had just had a conversation as a class about learning our addresses. We were reading *Jolly Post Man*, and we were looking at the addresses. Do you notice how much her writing looks like the addresses in the book, including the numbers going first?

• • • • • • • • • • • • • • • •

Sharing Progress With School Administrators

Center directors, principals, central-office administrators (e.g., the superintendent, the preschool center's advisory board, the school board, the language-arts supervisor), and state and federal agencies also want to know about the progress that all the children in each classroom or school are making toward the defined standards, outcomes, or goals. A data-collection form is often created, on which classroom teachers can summarize their students' portfolio information and arrive at a conclusion about how their students are progressing as a group. An example of such a form is presented in Figure 38. Using the information on this form, it is possible to aggregate the data across all children in a classroom or the school. Comparing the

Figure 38
Semester Development

Column 1: September
Column 2: December
Key: 1–3 = hears rhymes consistently
Key: 1–3 = sees written rime

Name	Hears Rhyming Words		Recognizes Written Rime	
Barry	2	3	1	3
Sheila	1	3	2	3
Celina	1	2	2	3

data from the fall to the spring permits school administrators to see changes in the percentages of children in each category within each teacher's classroom, within each grade level, and within the school who have met the standard or achieved the goal. Central-office administrators can calculate this information across all schools in the district. In this way, the portfolio data can become an integral component of the school's and the school district's accountability system.

This can then be translated into percentages, for example, in a class of 20 children. At the beginning of the year only 20% were able to consistently hear rhymes, but now at the end of the semester, 90% of the children are consistently able to identify rhyming words.

Influential professional associations such as NAEYC, the National Association of Early Childhood Specialists in State Departments of Education, and IRA have issued statements on assessment as an integral part of curriculum and instruction; however, the assessment of young children must be done in thoughtful ways in which their performance is sampled in the course of learning activities.

PROFESSIONAL DEVELOPMENT

One way teachers determine what they want and need to know about children's literacy development is by reviewing national, state, and local standards. Search your state's website or contact the state or a school district to obtain a copy of the state or local standards for language arts.

Develop a unit assessment checklist. Try collecting information for several days focusing on just a few children. Organize this information in a portfolio. What have these children learned? How would you share this information with parents?

CHAPTER 9

Including Families

Family members are children's first teachers, and they are the teachers that children have for the longest period of time. Quality early childhood programs in print- or literacy-rich environments engage family members as an integral part of the language and literacy programs in school and at home. All children are likely to become more successful readers and writers when teachers include strong **parent-involvement programs** in their literacy programs (Wasik, 2004).

Activities for Involving Families

In addition to participating in such activities as back-to-school nights, coming to watch their children perform in school programs, bringing cupcakes for birthday parties, helping on class trips, and running off blackline masters, parents must be informed about the literacy program and how they can help at home and in school. Equally important, teachers need to learn about children's home lives and literacy experiences from their parents.

Parents should come to school during the day to observe the program, to read to children, to share their cultural backgrounds and special skills, to help make center materials, and to supervise during center time. Working parents should be able to spend an hour twice a year if they are given a variety of times during which they can come to school. A newsletter should go to families once a month to keep them informed about what is happening in school, what they can send to school to help, and what they can do in school to help. Families must feel welcome in school and as partners in the education of their children. The following are tips and activities teachers can provide to help parents help their children develop literacy:

1. Provide a monthly newsletter about literacy-related activities in school.

2. Ask parents to participate in literacy-related activities in school, such as reading to children, sharing information about hobbies,

jobs, and cultural traditions, and coming to school to help at center time so teachers can work with individual children.

3. Have a workshop for parents to discuss activities in the school literacy program and what they can do at home to help.

4. Provide a list for parents with suggestions of books to buy for their home libraries or to borrow from the public library.

5. Encourage parents to have a place for books at home, even if it is only a cardboard box.

6. Encourage parents to provide children with a table to write on and writing materials, such as paper, pencils, and markers.

7. Encourage families to eat meals together and discuss the happenings of the day.

8. Encourage families to make regular errands such as going to the grocery store a literacy experience by having a child make a list of food items and check them off as they are picked up at the store.

9. Involve family members in discussing student progress.

10. Be in touch with families by way of e-mails, notes sent home, and phone calls. Try to make these communications positive, not negative.

Respecting Different Cultural Backgrounds in Children and Their Families

It is crucial that teachers show that they respect the cultural heritage and value the native languages of their students and their families from the moment the students walk into their classrooms. Imagine how scary it is for a young child to come into a place where everyone speaks a different language. Teachers should show interest in their students' native languages and try to learn at least a few key phrases in each of the languages represented in their classrooms (Xu, 2003). It is helpful to talk with parents about their child's level of familiarity with English. Teachers can invite parents to bring a translator to their initial conference or provide one if the parents wish. Whenever possible, schools should consider the parents' preference for their child's literacy instruction to determine whether the child should be taught with English-only instruction or in the family's primary language (IRA, 2001). Parents should be encouraged to participate in the classroom as much as possible, and to share their culture and language with their child's class.

The classroom should have plenty of texts in the native languages of ELLs. These include translations of favorite books, newspapers, menus, and other everyday texts that a student might encounter at home. Teachers should do everything they can to create a connection between each child's home and school literacy experiences. This is especially challenging because different cultures and communities embrace different approaches to literacy (Xu, 2003). Again, communication with parents about their children's home literacy practices will help teachers to improve instruction with ELLs. A teacher can also ask parents to introduce new concepts from the classroom in the child's native language, further enhancing the connection between home and school. If teachers become familiar with their students' cultures, the teachers are more likely to respond effectively to the students' needs. In some cultures, for example, children are encouraged to participate in classroom discussions; in others, children are encouraged not to speak in class. If we don't know the cultural traditions, we might interpret a child's behavior as rude or indifferent. Therefore, it is crucial to understand the behaviors of the children in our classrooms to respond to them in an appropriate manner (Hadaway & Young, 2006).

The questionnaire in Figure 39 should be helpful in getting information from parents about their children that will provide you with information that will help you better understand their culture and make the child and his or her family feel more comfortable in your classroom.

PROFESSIONAL DEVELOPMENT

Parents are crucial to the development of their children's literacy. Be sure to include parents by sending home newsletters on a regular basis to let them know what you are doing in school and what they can do to support your instruction. Extend many invitations for them to participate in the classroom or to simply observe. If they don't respond, make a telephone call to inform them of the latest developments. Meet with other teachers to share ideas on how to involve parents and collaborate on efforts. Parents need to be welcomed and their talents utilized. Make school a place they feel they can come for information and to help.

Figure 39
Helping Me Learn About You and Your Child

Child's name: _____

Father's name: _____ Father's country of origin: _____

Mother's name: _____ Mother's country of origin: _____

What name do you use for your child?

Does your child's name have a particular meaning or translation?

Where was your child born? Where else has you child lived and when?

How long has your family lived in [name your community]?

What language or languages do you use to speak to your child?
Father: _____ Mother: _____

What languages do you speak?
Father: _____ Mother: _____

Who are the immediate members of your family that your child lives with or spends a lot of time with, such as siblings, grandparents, aunts, uncles, cousins? List on the back of this form:
    Name   Relationship   Language used with your child

If English isn't your home language, about how many English words does your child know? (Circle 1)
    Fewer than 10   10 to 50   50 to 100   More than 100

If you belong to a particular religion, respond yes or no. If you wish, you can list the religion.

List the food that your child usually eats and likes.

List the food that your child cannot eat because of religious or other reasons.

What food does your child not like to eat?

What does your child usually eat with?
    a. Fingers   b. Chopsticks   c. Fork and spoon

Complete the sentences:
    When my child is with a group of children, I would expect my child to _____.
    When my child is misbehaving in class, I would expect the teacher to _____.
    If my child is unhappy in class, I would expect the teacher to _____.
    The three most important things my child could learn in school this year would be _____.

Note. Adapted by permission from Tabors, P.O. (1997). *One Child, Two Languages*. Baltimore: Paul H. Brookes.

REFERENCES

Adams, M.J. (1990). *Beginning to read: Thinking and learning about print.* Cambridge, MA: MIT Press.

Adams, M.J., Beeler, T., Foorman, B.R., & Lundberg, I. (1998). *Phonemic awareness in young children: A classroom curriculum.* Baltimore: Paul H. Brookes.

Airasian, P. (2002). *Assessment in the classroom.* New York: McGraw-Hill.

Allen, R. (1976). *Language experiences in communication.* Boston: Houghton Mifflin.

Anderson, R.C., Hiebert, E.H., Scott, J.A., & Wilkinson, I.A.G. (1985). *Becoming a nation of readers.* Washington, DC: U.S. Department of Education.

Applebee, A.N., & Langer, J.A. (1983). Instructional scaffolding: Reading and writing as natural language activities. *Language Arts, 60*(2), 168–175.

Armbruster, B.B., Lehr, F., & Osborn, J. (2001). *Put reading first: The research building blocks for teaching children to read.* Washington, DC: Partnership for Reading.

Au, K.H. (1998). Constructivist approaches, phonics, and the literacy learning of students of diverse backgrounds. In T. Shanahan & F.V. Rodriguez-Brown (Eds.), *47th yearbook of the National Reading Conference* (pp. 1–21). Chicago: National Reading Conference.

Baumann, J.F. (1992). Effect of think-aloud instruction on elementary students' comprehension monitoring abilities. *Journal of Reading Behavior, 24*(2), 143–172.

Beck, I.L., & McKeown, M.G. (2001). Text talks: Capturing the benefits of read-aloud experiences for young children. *The Reading Teacher, 55*(1), 10–20.

Berk, L. (1997). *Child development.* Boston: Allyn & Bacon.

Bloom, L. (1990). Development in express: Affect and speech. In N. Stein & T. Trabasso (Eds.), *Psychological and biological approaches to emotion* (pp. 215–245). Hillsdale, NJ: Erlbaum.

Brown, R., Cazden, C., & Bellugi-Klima, U. (1968). The child's grammar from one to three. In J.P. Hill (Ed.), *Minnesota symposium on child development* (pp. 28–73). Minneapolis, MI: University of Minneapolis Press.

Bryant, P.E., MacLean, M., Bradley, L.L., & Crossland, J. (1990). Rhyme and alliteration, phoneme detection, and learning to read. *Developmental Psychology, 26*(3), 429–438. doi:10.1037/0012-1649.26.3.429

Burns, M.S., Snow, C.E., & Griffin, P. (Eds.). (1999). *Starting out right: A guide to promoting children's reading success.* Washington, DC: National Academy Press.

Cazden, C.B. (2005). The value of conversations for language development and reading comprehension. *Literacy Teaching and Learning, 9*(1), 1–6.

Chall, J.S., Jacobs, V.A., & Baldwin, L.W. (1990). *The reading crisis: Why poor children fall behind.* Cambridge, MA: Harvard University Press.

Chard, D.J., Simmons, D.C., & Kameenui, E.J. (1998). Word recognition: Research bases. In D.C. Simmons & E.J. Kameenui (Eds.), *What reading research tells us about children with diverse learning needs: Bases and basics* (pp. 141–168). Mahwah, NJ: Erlbaum.

Christie, J., Enz, B.J., & Vukelich, C. (2006). *Teaching language and literacy: Preschool through the elementary grades* (3rd ed.). New York: Allyn & Bacon.

Clay, M. (1972). *Reading: The patterning of complex behaviour.* London: Heinemann.

Clay, M. (1975). *What did I write?* Auckland, New Zealand: Heinemann.

Committee on Education and the Workforce. (1999). *Literacy: Why children can't read: A review of current federal programs. Teachers: The key to helping America learn to read.* Hearing before the Committee on Education and the Workforce, House of Representatives, 105th Congress, first session, July 10, July 31, September 3, 1997, Washington, DC. Washington, DC: U.S. Government Printing Office.

Cosgrove, M.S. (1989). Read out loud? Why bother? *New England Reading Association Journal, 25,* 9–22.

Cox, C. (2002). *Teaching language arts: A student- and response-centered classroom* (4th ed.). Boston: Allyn & Bacon.

Cullinan, B.E. (1987). *Children's literature in the reading program.* Newark, DE: International Reading Association.

Cullinan, B.E. (1992). *Invitation to read: More children's literature in the reading program.* Newark, DE: International Reading Association.

Cunningham, A.E. (1990). Explicit versus implicit instruction in phonemic awareness. *Journal of Experimental Child Psychology, 50*(3), 429–444. doi:10.1016/0022-0965(90)90079-N

Dickinson, D.K., McCabe, A., Anastaspoulos, L., Peisner Feinberg, E.S., & Poe, M.D. (2003). The comprehensive language approach to early literacy: The interrelationships among vocabulary, phonological sensitivity, and print knowledge among preschool-aged children. *Journal of Educational Psychology, 95*(3), 465–481. doi:10.1037/0022-0663.95.3.465

Dickinson, D.K., & Tabors, P.O. (Eds.). (2001). *Beginning literacy with language.* Baltimore: Paul H. Brookes.

Dodge, D.T., Heroman, C., Charles, J., & Maiorca, J. (2004). Beyond outcomes, how ongoing assessment supports children's learning and leads to meaningful curriculum. *Young Children, 59*(1), 20–28.

Durkin, D. (1978/1979). What classroom observations reveal about reading instruction. *Reading Research Quarterly, 14*(4), 481–533. doi:10.1598/RRQ.14.4.2

Ehri, L.C. (1998). Research on learning to read and spell: A personal historical perspective. *Scientific Studies of Reading, 2*(2), 97–114. doi:10.1207/s1532799xssr0202_1

Elley, W. (1989). Vocabulary acquisition from listening to stories. *Reading Research Quarterly, 24*(2), 174–187. doi:10.2307/747863

Enz, B.J. (2006). Phonemic awareness. In C. Cummins (Ed.), *Understanding and implementing Reading First initiatives: The changing role of administrators* (pp. 18–30). Newark, DE: International Reading Association.

Enz, B.J., & Foley, D. (in press). Sharing a language and literacy legacy: A middle-class family's experience. In G. Li (Ed.), *Multicultural families, home literacies, and mainstream schooling* (pp. 153–174). New York: SUNY Press.

Enz, B.J., Kortman, S., & Honaker, C. (2008). *Managing the classroom: Primary and elementary grades.* Dubuque, IA: Kendall-Hunt.

Enz, B.J., Gerard, M., Han, M., & Prior, J. (2008). Exploring intentional instructional uses of environmental print in preschool and primary grades. In A.D.-B. Parecki (Ed.), *Effective early literacy practice: Here's how, here's why* (pp. 76–90). Ypsilanti, MI: High Scope Press.

Ferreiro, E., & Teberosky, A. (1982). *Literacy before schooling.* Exeter, NH: Heinemann.

Freeman, D., & Freeman, Y. (1993). Strategies for promoting the primary languages of all students. *The Reading Teacher, 46*(7), 18–25.

Froebel, F. (1974). *The education of man.* Clifton, NJ: August A. Kelly.

Gambrell, L., Pfeiffer, W., & Wilson, R. (1985). The effect of retelling upon comprehension and recall of text information. *The Journal of Educational Research, 78*(4), 216–220.

Gaskins, I.W. (2003). A multidimensional approach to beginning literacy. In D.M. Barone & L.M. Morrow (Eds.), *Literacy and young children: Research-based practices* (pp. 45–60). New York: Guilford.

Genishi, C., & Dyson, A. (1984). *Language assessment in the early years.* Norwood, NJ: Ablex.

Goodman, Y. (1986). Children coming to know literacy. In W. Teale & E. Sulzby (Eds.), *Emergent literacy: Writing and reading* (pp. 1–14). Norwood, NJ: Ablex.

Graves, M.F., Juel, C., & Graves, B.B. (1998). *Teaching reading in the 21st century.* Boston: Allyn & Bacon.

Gump, P.V. (1989). Ecological psychology and issues of play. In M.N. Bloch & D. Pellegrini (Eds.), *The ecological context of children's play* (pp. 35–56). Norwood, NJ: Ablex.

Gunning, T.G. (2003). *Creating literacy instruction for all children* (4th ed.). Boston: Allyn & Bacon.

Hadaway, N.L., & Young, T.A. (2006). Changing classrooms: Transforming instruction. In T.A. Young & N.L. Hadaway (Eds.), *Supporting the literacy development of English learners: Increasing success in all classrooms* (pp. 6–21). Newark, DE: International Reading Association.

Halliday, M.A.K. (1975). *Learning how to mean: Exploration in the development of language.* London: Edward Arnold.

Harste, J., Woodward, V., & Burke, C. (1984). *Language stories and literacy lessons.* Portsmouth, NH: Heinemann.

Hart, B., & Risley, T.R. (1999). *The social world of children learning to talk.* Baltimore: Paul H. Brookes.

Hatcher, P., Hulme, C., & Ellis, A. (1994). Ameliorating reading failure by integrating the teaching of reading and phonological skills: The phonological linkage hypothesis. *Child Development, 65*(1), 41–57. doi:10.2307/1131364

Holdaway, D. (1979). *The foundations of literacy.* Sydney: Ashton Scholastic.

Holmes, R., & Cunningham, B. (1995). Young children's knowledge of their classrooms: Names, activities, and purposes of learning centers. *Education & Treatment of Children, 18*(4), 433–443.

Hunt, K.W. (1970). *Syntactic maturity in children and adults. Monograph of the Society for Research in Child Development* (Vol. 25). Chicago: University of Chicago Press.

Hurford, D.P., Darrow, L., Edwards, T., Howerton, C., Mote, C., Schauf, J., et al. (1993). An examination of phonemic processing abilities in children during their first-grade year. *Journal of Learning Disabilities, 26*(3), 167–177.

International Reading Association. (1999). *Using multiple methods of beginning reading instruction* (Position statement). Newark, DE: Author.

International Reading Association. (2001, April/May). Association issues position statement on second-language literacy instruction. *Reading Today, 18*(5), 6.

International Reading Association & National Association for the Education of Young Children. (1998). *Learning to read and write: Developmentally appropriate practices for young children.* Newark, DE; Washington, DC: Authors.

International Reading Association & National Council of Teachers of English. (1994). *Standards for the assessment of reading and writing.* Newark, DE; Urbana, IL: Authors.

Jewell, M., & Zintz, M. (1986). *Learning to read naturally.* Dubuque, IA: Kendall/Hunt.

Kershner, R., & Pointon, P. (2000). Children's views of the primary classroom as an environment for working and learning. *Research in Education, 64,* 64–78.

Kuhl, P. (1994). Learning and representation in speech and language. *Current Opinion in Neurobiology, 4,* 812–822. doi:10.1016/0959-4388(94)90128-7

Leu, D.J., & Kinzer, C. (1991). *Effective reading instruction K–8* (2nd ed.). New York: Merrill.

Liberman, I.Y., Shankweiler, D., & Liberman, A.M. (1989). The alphabetic principle and learning to read. In D. Shankweiler & I.Y. Liberman (Eds.), *Phonology and reading disability: Solving the reading puzzle* (pp. 1–33). Ann Arbor: University of Michigan Press.

Lindfors, J. (1989). The classroom: A food environment for language learning. In P. Rigg & V. Allen (Eds.), *When they don't all speak English: Integrating the ESL student into the regular classroom* (pp. 39–54). Urbana, IL: National Council of Teachers of English.

Loughlin, C.E., & Martin, M.D. (1987). *Supporting literacy: Developing effective learning environments.* New York: Teachers College Press.

Mann, V.A. (1993). Phoneme awareness and future reading ability. *Journal of Learning Disabilities, 26*(4), 259–269.

McGee, L. (2007). Language and literacy assessment in preschool. In J. Paratore & R. McCormack (Eds.), *Classroom literacy assessment: Making sense of what students know and do* (pp. 65–84). New York: Guilford.

McGee, L., & Richgels, D. (1989). "K is Kristen's": Learning the alphabet from a child's perspective. *The Reading Teacher, 43*(3), 216–225.

Miramontes, O.B., Nadeau, A., & Commins, N.L. (1997). *Reconstructing schools for linguistic diversity: Linking decision making to effective programs.* New York: Teachers College Press.

Montessori, M. (1965). *Spontaneous activity in education*. New York: Schocken Books.

Moore, G. (1986). Effects of the spatial definition of behavior settings on children's behavior: A quasi-experimental field study. *Journal of Environmental Psychology, 6*(3), 205–231. doi:10.1016/S0272-4944(86)80023-8

Morrow, L.M. (1978). Analysis of syntax in the language of six-, seven-, and eight-year-olds. *Research in the Teaching of English, 12*(2), 143–148.

Morrow, L.M. (1983). Home and school correlates of early interest in literature. *The Journal of Educational Research, 76*(4), 221–230.

Morrow, L.M. (1984). Reading stories to young children: Effects of story structure and traditional questioning strategies on comprehension. *Journal of Reading Behavior, 16*, 273–288.

Morrow, L.M. (1985). Retelling stories: A strategy for improving children's comprehension, concept of story structure and oral language complexity. *The Elementary School Journal, 85*(5), 647–661. doi:10.1086/461427

Morrow, L.M. (1988). Young children's responses to one-to-one story readings in school settings. *Reading Research Quarterly, 23*(1), 89–107. doi:10.2307/747906

Morrow, L.M. (1990). Preparing the classroom environment to promote literacy during play. *Early Childhood Research Quarterly, 5*(4), 537–554. doi:10.1016/0885-2006(90)90018-V

Morrow, L.M. (1996). Story retelling: A discussion strategy to develop and assess comprehension. In L.B. Gambrell & J.F. Almasi (Eds.), *Lively discussions: Fostering engaged reading* (pp. 265–285). Newark, DE: International Reading Association.

Morrow, L.M. (2002). *The literacy center: Contexts for reading and writing* (2nd ed.). York, ME: Stenhouse.

Morrow, L.M. (2005). *Literacy development in the early years: Helping children read and write* (5th ed.). Boston: Allyn & Bacon.

Morrow, L.M., Freitag, E., & Gambrell, L.B. (2009). *Using children's literature in preschool to develop comprehension: Understanding and enjoying books* (2nd ed.). Newark, DE: International Reading Association.

Morrow, L.M., Kuhn, M.R., & Schwanenflugel, P.J. (2006). The family fluency program. *The Reading Teacher, 60*(4), 322–333. doi:10.1598/RT.60.4.2

Morrow, L.M., & Rand, M. (1991). Promoting literacy during play by designing early childhood classroom environments. *The Reading Teacher, 44*(6), 396–405.

National Association for the Education of Young Children & National Association of Early Childhood Specialists in State Departments of Education. (2004). Where we stand: On curriculum, assessment, and program evaluation. *Young Children, 59*(1), 51–54. Available at www.naeyc.org/about/positions/pdf/StandlCurrAss.pdf

National Institute of Child Health and Human Development. (2000). *Report of the National Reading Panel. Teaching children to read: An evidence-based assessment of the scientific research literature on reading and its implications for reading instruction* (NIH Publication No. 00-4769). Washington, DC: U.S. Government Printing Office.

Neuman, S.B., & Roskos, K. (1992). Literacy objects as cultural tools: Effects on children's literacy behaviors in play. *Reading Research Quarterly, 27*(3), 203–225. doi:10.2307/747792

Neuman, S.B., & Roskos, K. (1997). Literacy knowledge in practice: Contexts of participation for young writers and readers. *Reading Research Quarterly, 32*(1), 10–33. doi:10.1598/RRQ.32.1.2

Newberger, J.J. (1997). New brain development research: A wonderful window of opportunity to build public support for early childhood education. *Young Children, 52*(4), 4–9.

Olds, A.R. (1987). Designing settings for infants and toddlers. In C.S. Weinstein & T.G. David (Eds.), *Spaces for children: The built environment and child development* (pp. 117–138). New York: Plenum Press.

Otto, B. (2006) *Language development in early childhood* (2nd ed.). Upper Saddle River, NJ: Merrill/Prentice Hall.

Pearson, P.D., Roehler, L.R., Dole, J.A., & Duffy, G.G. (1992). Developing expertise in reading comprehension. In S.J. Samuels & A.E. Farstrup (Eds.), *What research has to say about reading instruction* (2nd ed., pp. 145–199). Newark, DE: International Reading Association.

Pellegrini, A., & Galda, L. (1982). The effects of thematic fantasy play training on the development of children's story comprehension. *American Educational Research Journal, 19*(3), 443–452.

Pflaum, S. (1986). *The development of language and literacy in young children* (3rd ed.). Columbus, OH: Merrill.

Pressley, M., & Afflerbach, P. (1995). *Verbal protocols of reading: The nature of constructively responsive reading.* Hillsdale, NJ: Erlbaum.

Pressley, M., & Hilden, K. (2002). How can children be taught to comprehend text better? In M.L. Kamil, J.B. Manning, & H.J. Walberg (Eds.), *Successful reading instruction* (pp. 33–53). Greenwich, CT: Information Age Publishing.

Pressley, M., Rankin, J., & Yokoi, L. (1996). A survey of the instructional practices of outstanding primary-level literacy teachers. *The Elementary School Journal, 96*(4), 363–384. doi:10.1086/461834

Prior, J., & Gerard, M. (2004). *Environmental print in the classroom: Meaningful connections for learning to read.* Newark, DE: International Reading Association.

RAND Reading Study Group. (2002). *Reading for understanding: Toward an R&D program in reading comprehension.* Santa Monica, CA: RAND.

Rasinski, T. (1990). Effects of repeated reading and listening-while-reading on reading fluency. *The Journal of Educational Research, 83*(3), 147–150.

Read, C. (1971). Pre-school children's knowledge of English phonology. *Harvard Educational Review, 41*(1), 1–34.

Ritchie, S., James-Szanton, J., & Howes, C. (2003). Emergent literacy practices in early childhood classrooms. In C. Howes (Ed.), *Teaching 4- to 8- year-olds: Literacy, math, multiculturalism, and classroom community* (pp. 71–92). Baltimore: Paul H. Brookes.

Rivilin, L., & Weinstein, C.S. (1984). Educational issues, school settings, and environ-mental psychology. *Journal of Environmental Psychology, 4*(4), 347–364. doi:10.1016/S0272-4944(84)80005-5

Ruddell, R.B., & Ruddell, M.R. (1995). *Teaching children to read and write: Becoming an influential teacher.* Boston: Allyn & Bacon.

Rusk, R., & Scotland, J. (1979). *Doctrines of the great educators.* New York: St. Martin's Press.

Seefeldt, C., & Barbour, N. (1986). *Early childhood education: An introduction.* Columbus, OH: Merrill.

Shaywitz, S. (2003). *Overcoming dyslexia.* New York: Alfred A. Knopf.

Shepard, L., Kagan, S., & Wurtz, E. (1998). Goal 1 early childhood assessments re-source group recommends. *Young Children, 53*(3), 52–54.

Shore, K. (2001, March). Success for ESL students: 12 practical tips to help second-language learners. *Instructor, 110*(6), 30–32.

Snider, V.E. (1995). A primer on phonemic awareness: What it is, why it's important, and how to teach it. *School Psychology Review, 24*(3), 443–455.

Snow, C.E., Burns, M.S., & Griffin, P. (Eds.). (1998). *Preventing reading difficulties in young children.* Washington, DC: National Academy Press.

Spector, J.E. (1995). Phonemic awareness training: Application of principles of direct instruction. *Reading and Writing Quarterly: Overcoming Learning Difficulties, 11*(1), 37–52.

Stanovich, K.E. (1986). Matthew effects in reading: Some consequences of individual differences in the acquisition of literacy. *Reading Research Quarterly, 21*(4), 360–407. doi:10.1598/RRQ.21.4.1

Stanovich, K.E. (1993/1994). Romance and reality (Distinguished Educator Series). *The Reading Teacher, 47*(4), 280–291.

Stauffer, R.G. (1980). *The language-experience approach to the teaching of reading* (2nd ed.). New York: Harper & Row.

Sulzby, E. (1985). Children's emergent reading of favorite storybooks: A developmen-tal study. *Reading Research Quarterly, 20*(4), 458–481. doi:10.1598/RRQ.20.4.4

Sulzby, E. (1990). Assessment of emergent writing and children's language while writ-ing. In L.M. Morrow & J.K. Smith (Eds.), *Assessment for instruction in early literacy* (pp. 83–108). Englewood Cliffs, NJ: Prentice Hall.

Sulzby, E., & Barnhart, J. (1990). The developing kindergartner: All of our children emerge as writers and readers. In J. McKee (Ed.), *The developing kindergarten: Programs, children, and teachers* (pp. 169–189). Ann Arbor: Michigan Association for the Education of Young Children.

Sulzby, E., Barnhart, J., & Hieshima, J. (1989). Forms of writing and rereading from writing: A preliminary report. In J. Mason (Ed.), *Reading and writing connections* (pp. 31–63). Boston: Allyn & Bacon.

Sulzby, E., & Teale, W.H. (1987). *Young children's storybook reading: Hispanic and Anglo families and children* (Report to the Spencer Foundation). Ann Arbor: University of Michigan.

Tabors, P.O. (1997). *One child, two languages.* Baltimore: Paul H. Brookes.

Taylor, N.E., Blum, I.H., & Logsdon, D.M. (1986). The development of written language awareness: Environmental aspects and program characteristics. *Reading Research Quarterly, 21*(2), 132–149. doi:10.2307/747841

Teale, W.H. (1984). Reading to young children: Its significance for literacy development. In H. Goelman, A. Oberg, & F. Smith (Eds.), *Awakening to literacy* (pp. 110–121). Exeter, NH: Heinemann.

Veatch, J., Sawicki, F., Elliot, G., Flake, E., & Blakey, J. (1979). *Key words to reading: The language experience approach begins.* Columbus, OH: Merrill.

Vukelich, C., & Christie, J. (2009). *Building a foundation for preschool literacy: Effective instruction for children's reading and writing development* (2nd ed.). Newark, DE: International Reading Association.

Vukelich, C., Christie, J., & Enz, B.J. (2007). *Helping young children learn language and literacy* (2nd ed.). New York: Allyn & Bacon.

Wasik, B. (Ed.). (2004). *Handbook of family literacy.* Mahwah, NJ: Erlbaum.

Weinstein, C.S. (1981). Classroom design as an external condition for learning. *Educational Technology, 21*(8), 12–19.

Weinstein, C.S., & Mignano, A.J., Jr. (1996). *Elementary classroom management.* New York: McGraw-Hill.

Wolfersberger, M., Reutzel, D.R., Sudweeks, R., & Fawson, P.F. (2004). Developing and validating the Classroom Literacy Environmental Profile (CLEP): A tool for examining the "print richness" of classrooms. *Journal of Literacy Research, 36*(2), 211–272.

Xu, H. (2003). The learner, the teacher, the text, and the context: Sociocultural approaches to early literacy instruction for English language learners. In D.M. Barone & L.M. Morrow (Eds.), *Literacy and young children: Research-based practices* (pp. 61–80). New York: Guilford.

Yopp, H.K. (1992). Developing phonemic awareness in young children. *The Reading Teacher, 45*(9), 696–703.

Young, T.A., & Hadaway, N.L. (Eds.) *Supporting the literacy development of English learners: Increasing success in all classrooms* (pp. 6–18). Newark, DE: International Reading Association.

CHILDREN'S LITERATURE CITED

Bourgeois, P. (1987). *Franklin in the dark.* New York: Scholastic.

Brenner, B. (1973). *The three little pigs.* New York: Random House.

Brown, M. (1957). *The three billy goats gruff.* New York: Harcourt.

Carle, E. (1969). *The very hungry caterpillar.* New York: Philomel.

Carle, E. (1985). *The very busy spider.* New York: Philomel.

Eastman, P.D. (1960). *Are you my mother?* New York: Random House.

Hall, Z. (1998). *The surprise garden.* New York: Scholastic.

Hennesy, B.G. (1990). *Jake baked the cake.* New York: Viking Penguin.

Hoberman, M.A., & Westcott, N.B. (2004). *I know an old lady who swallowed a fly.* New York: Little, Brown.

Izawa, T. (1986). *Goldilocks and the three bears.* New York: Grosset & Dunlap.

Kasza, K. (1988). *The pigs' picnic.* New York: G.P. Putnam's Sons.

Keats, E.J. (1966). *Jenny's hat.* New York: Viking.

Keats, E.J. (1967). *Peter's chair.* New York: Harper & Row.

Lionni, L. (1963). *Swimmy.* New York: Knopf.

Numeroff, L. (1985). *If you give a mouse a cookie.* New York: HarperCollins.

Sendak, M. (1963). *Where the wild things are.* New York: Harper & Row.

Seuss, D. (1960). *Green eggs and ham.* New York: Random House.

Willems, M. (2004). *Knuffle bunny.* New York: Hyperion.

Wood, A. (1982). *Quick as a cricket.* Singapore: Child's Play.

Wybow, T. (2002). *Life cycle of a frog.* New York: Crabtree.

Zolotow, C. (1962). *Mr. Rabbit and the lovely present.* New York: HarperCollins.

INDEX

Note: Page numbers followed by *f* and *t* indicate figures and tables, respectively.

F

G

H

L

M

Mote, C., 58, 74

multiple assessments for preschoolers, 1–9; frequently used types of assessment, 3–4; frequently use types of testing, 4–5; overview of assessment strategies, 6–9; standardized testing concerns, 5–6

N

Nadeu, A., 55

names: attendance taking with name cards and syllable-clap, 64–65; children's, 23, 25, 54, 78, 83; helper charts, 80; sign-up and take turns lists, 80–81

National Association for the Education of Young Children, 7, 14, 130, 136; *Learning to Read and Write: Developmentally Appropriate Practices for Young Children,* 7–8, 119

National Association of Early Childhood Specialists in State Departments of Education, 130, 136

National Council of Teachers of English, 119

National Institute of Child Health and Human Development, 58, 59, 74

National Reading Panel, 77, 96

National Institute of Education, 97–98

Neuman, S.B., 22, 52

neuron shearing in the brain, 48

Newberger, J.J., 39

No Child Left Behind Act, 2

nonfiction books, 53, 109

nonsense words, 38, 68

norm-referenced tests, 43; definition of, 4. *See also* tests and testing

numeric score or grade, 2

Numeroff, L., 91

O

Olds, A.R., 22

on-demand tests: definition of, 3. *See also* assessment

one-on-one basis, 56; in assessment, 104–108; in comprehension, 104, 108, 114

on-going assessment, 72, 119; definition of, 3. *See also* assessment

onsets: definition of, 3; teaching and assessing, 66–69, 69*f*, 70*f*

Osborn, J., 58

Otto, B., 41

P

parent-involvement programs: definition of, xi. *See also* families

parents: and medical referrals, 74; reading to children, 77; sharing data with, 122*f*–123*f*, 131–135, 133*f*, 134*f*; showcase portfolios for, 4, 124, 128. *See also* families

Peabody Picture Vocabulary Test (PPVT III) Expressive Vocabulary, 47

Pearson, P.D., 98

Peisner–Feinberg, E.S., 35

Pellegrini, A., 110

percentile ranks, 4–5

person function of language, 37

Pfeiffer, W., 109

Pflaum, S., 37

phonemes, 47, 58, 69; definition of, xi

phonemic awareness: definition of, xi

phonics: definition of, ix, 2, 58; initial instruction in, 66